Praise For Jackson I

Over 100 ★★★★★ reviews on the most tr(
International #1 Best Sellin(

"[Jackson Dean Chase is] **a fresh and powerful new voice.**"
—Terry Trueman, Printz Honor author of *Stuck in Neutral*

"[Chase] **grabs readers from page one.**"
—Nate Philbrick, author of *The Little One*

Praise for How to Start Your Novel

"**Writers of every genre will benefit** from this book."
—*Kindle reviewer*

"**...You'll never look at opening lines the same way again.**"
—*Kindle reviewer*

Praise for the How to Write Realistic Fiction Series

"This is **a must-have** that **will pay for itself many times over.**"
—Kindle reviewer

"**I can't imagine not using this book** the next time I write a story."
—Kindle reviewer

Praise for the Writers' Phrase Books Series

"**Every writer should own this guide . . .**"
—Derek Aisles, author of *Zombie Command*

". . . It's **worth your investment.**"
—Lake Lopez, author of *Thorns in Dark Places*

"**...Made me feel even I could write a book** . . . [These guides show you how] to grab a reader's attention and hold it."
—Tome Tender

"**...This book has helped me tremendously.** I was ready to trash my manuscript and now I'm halfway through editing the first draft!"
—Kindle reviewer

BOOKS BY JACKSON DEAN CHASE

Non-Fiction

How to Write Realistic Fiction series:
#1 How to Write Realistic Characters
#2 How to Write Realistic Men

Story Secrets for Writers series:
#1 How to Start Your Novel

Writers' Phrase Books series:
#1 Horror Writers' Phrase Book
#2 Post-Apocalypse Writers' Phrase Book
#3 Action Writers' Phrase Book
#4 Fantasy Writers' Phrase Book
#5 Fiction Writers' Phrase Book (series sampler)
#6 Science Fiction Writers' Phrase Book
#7 Romance, Emotion, and Erotica Writer's Phrase Book

Fiction

Beyond the Dome series:
#0 Hard Times in Dronetown
#1 Drone

Young Adult Horror series:
#1 Come to the Cemetery
#2 The Werewolf Wants Me
#3 The Haunting of Hex House
#4 Gore Girls: Twisted Tales & Poems
#5 Lost Girls: Twisted Tales & Poems
#6 Horror Girls: Twisted Tales & Poems
#7 Killer Young Adult Fiction (complete series + extras)

Poetry

Raw Underground Poetry series:
#1 Bukowski's Ghost
#2 Love at the Bottom of the Litter Box
#3 Christmas Eve in the Drunk Tank
#4 Be the Magic
#5 Death of a Scratching Post

Romance

Emotion & Erotica

WRITERS' PHRASE BOOK

Essential Reference and Thesaurus for Authors of All Romantic Fiction, including Contemporary, Historical, Paranormal, Science Fiction, and Suspense

JACKSON DEAN CHASE

www.JacksonDeanChase.com

LEGAL DISCLAIMER: Note that this book is not, and makes NO claim to be, the classic *Romance Writers' Phrase Book* (1984). It is NOT affiliated in any way with that groundbreaking book, its publisher, or its authors. It contains NO derivative material. This is a wholly separate and original work, created to aid modern writers looking to spice up their emotional, erotic, and romantic scenes regardless of genre.

— To love, passion, and the written word —

First Printing, July 2016
ISBN-13: 978-1535127226
ISBN-10: 1535127228

Published by Jackson Dean Chase, Inc.

Printed by CreateSpace

ROMANCE, EMOTION, AND EROTICA WRITERS' PHRASE BOOK

Copyright © 2016 Jackson Dean Chase, Inc. All rights reserved.

Cover art by SelfPubBookCovers.com/Shardel

Author photo by C. Graves. Copyright © 2015 Jackson Dean Chase, Inc.

Without limiting the rights under copyright above, no part of this book may be reproduced, stored in or introduced into a retrieval system or transmitted, in any form or by any means (electronic, mechanical, photocopying, recording, or otherwise), without the written consent of the copyright holder and publisher of this book.

PUBLISHER'S NOTES

"Bold Visions of Dark Places" is a trademark of Jackson Dean Chase, Inc.

All the material herein is presented "as is" with no warranty of fitness given for any specific purpose. Neither the author nor his affiliates, heirs, partners, or publishers assume any responsibility for errors, inaccuracies, or omissions.

The scanning, uploading, and distribution of this book via the Internet or via any other means without the written permission of the publisher is illegal and punishable by law. Please purchase only authorized electronic editions, and do not participate in or encourage electronic piracy of copyrighted materials. Your support is appreciated.

End User License Agreement (EULA): By purchasing this *Writers' Phrase Book*, you unconditionally accept and agree that the copyright holder is hereby granting you, the End User, a limited royalty free and non-transferrable license to copy and use the descriptive tags presented herein "as is" or modified however you like **for use in your own fiction only** and only for so long as you own this book. By using said tags in any capacity in your own work, you hereby acknowledge, attest, and agree that you will not violate the exclusive copyright and/or any other rights the copyright holder has over said tags, and to recognize that all other rights not expressly granted by this license are reserved by the copyright holder. You do not have permission to use said tags either in their original version or in modified form in a collection of tags and/or other writing advice or in any kind of standalone capacity, including but not limited to written or electronic. In other words, you cannot take the descriptive tags in this book and repurpose them into your own phrase book, thesaurus, word list, app, or for any other use in any format under any circumstances. If you are not the original purchaser of this book, **you must purchase your own copy to receive a valid license**; said copy must be bought new from the copyright holder directly or his authorized reseller(s). If you have questions about this Agreement, please contact the copyright holder.

Want FREE books? Visit the Author at:
www.JacksonDeanChase.com

Contents

WHO IS THIS BOOK FOR? 8
INTRODUCTION 9
Writing Exercises 46

PART 1: *Hearts and Minds*

EMOTIONS

Aloof, Annoyed, and Uncaring 12
Ambition and Greed 13
Dislike and Disgust 15
Embarrassment, Shame, and Surprise 16
Fear and Shock 17
Happiness and Flirtation 21
Hate and Revenge 22
Jealousy 27
Love and Romance 28
Sadness and Despair 30

PART 2: *Bodies & Souls*

ROMANCE AND EROTICA

Afterglow/Waking Up 34
Arousal, Lust, and Temptation 36
Bed 41
Body and Face Descriptions (Female) 42
Body and Face Descriptions (Male) 44
Body Heat 45
Bondage & Kink 46
Breasts 49
Breathing 52

Buttocks 53
Carrying 54
Clothes (Removal) 55
Eyes 52
Foreplay (Female on Male) 59
Foreplay (Male on Female) 62
Hair 64
Lips and Kisses 66
Mouth, Teeth, and Tongues 71
Orgasm and Pleasure (Female) 73
Orgasm and Pleasure (Male) 77
Orgasm and Pleasure (Mutual) 80
Penetration 81
Penetration (First Time) 87
Pregnancy 88
Protection 89
Scent 89
Sounds (Female) 91
Sounds (Male) 92
Sounds (Mutual) 93
Sweat 94
Touch (Misc.) 95

PART 3: *Paranormal & Fantasy Romance*
THINGS THAT GO HUMP IN THE NIGHT
Supernatural Creatures and Magic 102

PART 4: *Science Fiction Romance*
PLEASURE BEYOND SPACE AND TIME
Science Fiction and Time Travel Romance 124
Alien Creatures 126

PART 5: *Words of Passion*

BONUS MATERIAL

Action Vocabulary 140

Body Vocabulary 143

Emotion Vocabulary 144

Love's Coloring Book 148

Titles and Terms (for Fantasy, Historical, and Science Fiction) 150

WRITING ADVICE (BOXED TEXT)

Alpha and Beta Heroes 122

How to Divorce Yourself from Weak Writing 46

Limits of Magic 120

Romance Writing 101 99

Romance Writing Rules 18

Superlatives for Lovers 86

True Beauty Is Never Skin Deep 154

True Love Comes in Stages 138

Writing Effective Action Scenes 125

Writing Romantic Heroines and Heroes 113

Please Read Before Buying

The *Writers' Phrase Books* series are intended to be stand-alone volumes. As such, they contain a varying degree of overlapping content. If you are not writing cross-genre fiction, you may not need to own more than one.

The *Romance, Emotion, and Erotica Writers' Phrase Book* contains substantial new and revised content intended for all fiction authors, but especially those writing romance, including such categories as alien warrior romance, chick-lit, contemporary romance, erotica, erotic romance, hen-lit, historical romance, mom-lit, new adult, paranormal romance, romantic suspense, science fiction or futuristic romance, time travel romance, western romance, and women's fiction.

Due to frank and explicit descriptions of nudity and sex, **this book is intended for mature readers**, and those writing only sweet traditional, Regency, or inspirational romances may not find this book as useful as those writing other romantic categories.

Although there is **no specific LGBTQ content**, you can easily gender-swap most of the descriptions to create your own. Have fun!

Who Is This Book For?

This book isn't just for romance writers. It's for anyone who wants to **write emotional, sexy, or romantic scenes**, regardless of genre. Got a romance subplot or sex scene that needs spicing up? This book is for you! *Anyone can use it.*

That said, it's obviously going to be the best value for writers of:

- Chick-Lit / City Girl / Women's Fiction
- Contemporary Romance
- Erotic Romance / Romantica
- Erotica (Erotic Horror, etc.)
- Fantasy Romance
- Historical Romance
- New Adult
- Paranormal Romance
- Romantic Suspense
- Science Fiction Romance (Dystopian, Time Travel, etc.)

This book isn't designed to teach you how to plot your novel (it assumes you already know that). What it does do is teach you **how to quickly and easily write dramatic and powerful descriptions** for your characters' emotions and actions.

Although I include helpful material for most cross-genre romance and erotica authors, those of you requiring more action and world-building descriptions will want to take a look at the rest of my series:

- *Action Writers' Phrase Book*
- *Fantasy Writers' Phrase Book*
- *Fiction Writers' Phrase Book (series sampler)* *
- *Horror Writers' Phrase Book* **
- *Post-Apocalypse Writers' Phrase Book*
- *Science Fiction Writers' Phrase Book* ***

* This series sampler covers a variety of weapons, wounds, weather, and wildlife from the other books.

** This Romance book contains the complete Paranormal Romance section from the *Horror Writers' Phrase Book*—it has been substantially revised and expanded, along with providing additional descriptions for a broad sampling of supernatural lovers, from angels to werewolves.

** This Romance book contains the complete Aliens and Cyborgs section from the *Science Fiction Writers' Phrase Book*. The sections on Science Fiction and Time Travel Romance are new to this book.

Introduction

I'm going to tell you a secret: *A lot of what you write isn't what you say, it's how you say it.* Sure, characters, story structure, and dialogue are important. There are a ton of books written on those subjects for a reason. But you could be an expert in all those things and still fail to tell a compelling story.

Why? Well, to be a truly great writer, you must constantly find new ways to say the same old things. Let's say you're writing a novel about a a young couple falling in love. Maybe it's a romance, new adult, or erotica story. Maybe it's not. That doesn't matter. What does is you knowing a ton of different ways to describe how your characters feel and how they bond . . . including how they have sex. Remember, these things are going to come up dozens of times and you've got hundreds of pages to fill!

And here's the terrible trap so many authors fall into: Sooner or later, you end up writing the same lazy descriptions over and over. And you'll agonize over each and every one, wondering how to inject new energy into them. But what if you didn't have to suffer? What if you had an entire book of ready-made tags to inspire you at a moment's notice?

TAG — YOU'RE IT!

Wait! What are tags, you ask? Tags are short descriptive phrases peppered between the dialogue and strung throughout the narrative. Done with skill, the reader never notices them, but their dramatic resonance is deeply felt. Trust me, your readers will notice if they're missing or not up to snuff!

Consider the difference between saying, "He was madly in love with her" or "He burned with a heat that scorched his soul." Which do you prefer? Which is more exciting? Sure, both get the author's point across, but the second is more likely to leave the reader breathless and scrambling to turn the page.

Tags are like Cupid's arrows. They are the greatest weapons in a writer's arsenal. The more you have, the more excited and aroused you can make your readers. Isn't it time you broke up with boring lines and breathed new life into your characters and situations?

INSTANTLY WRITE BETTER ROMANCE & EROTICA

This power-packed book helps you write emotional, romantic, and sexy scenes for any genre, time period, or world.

Every story requires building the right atmosphere to create an emotional connection to its reader. Without one, why would anyone care to read about your hero or heroine?

In the best fiction, your hero or heroine becomes a stand-in for readers to project themselves into and identify with. Readers *want* to feel her fear, her hope, her struggle to find true love.

So how do we make our heroine more meaningful? We assign her thoughts, words, and actions greater power with every tap of our keyboard. In short, we punch her up with tags. And we do the same for the dashing hero, the villain, and everyone else who matters.

Use your intuition. Not every line needs to be punched-up. After all, sometimes it's perfectly fine (and perhaps even *more* dramatic in a minimalist sense) to say, "He loved her," instead of "His heart beat for her and no other."

Nor is it wise for every act, thought or description to be over-the-top or made to stick out unnecessarily. But when you want to really emphasize something, to build atmosphere and heighten emotion, nothing beats a well-written tag. Use them right, use them well, and your stories will never be the same.

How Do I Use This Book?

At the very least, just flipping through these pages should jumpstart your creative juices, especially if you've come down with a bad case of writer's block. You can use the tags as writing prompts to help you generate new scenes or even entire stories, but the most common method is to use them as quick "fill in the blanks" whenever you need a line. You have my permission to copy them "as is," or customize them however you like.

Some tags are more specific than others, so you may find it helpful to swap out whatever doesn't work for you with whatever you need. For example, changing the gender of the character and/or action is easily done, as is replacing the generic pronouns given with your character's names or some other vivid description instead (e.g., changing "he" to "the billionaire").

You can achieve a variety of exciting effects by mixing and matching tags (or parts of tags) from the same or different categories to create new ones. So you not only have all the individual tags as written, but you also have an incredible number of combinations—a number limited only by your imagination. There's no wrong way to use this book except not to use it all. *It's yours.* Feel free to tinker with it. Mark it up, write in the margins, but whatever you do, have fun!

Jackson Dean Chase

www.JacksonDeanChase.com

— Part 1 —
Hearts & Minds

— Emotions —

Aloof, Annoyed, and Uncaring

It seemed no kindness could bring a smile to his lips

His icy demeanor repelled her

His cold efficiency shocked her

He was cold, ruthless, with no spark of passion to guide him

He seemed closed to emotion and to love most of all

Her suggestion was met with a contemptuous snort

The billionaire acted as if she didn't exist

The aristocrat's response was a maddening smirk

He reacted with grim determination

His gaze was level, direct, and seemed to bore into her

He was beautiful, yes, but there was a coldness to him

He talked in a blunt style that grated on her nerves

An icy air of command hung about the noble lord

Here was a man who would brook no nonsense

He acted with a precise, machine-like efficiency

He was well-mannered, but without compassion

Now that cold gaze of his was leveled on her and she shrank from it

He took an aggressive step forward as if what she wanted didn't matter

He raised an untamed brow in annoyance

He replied with a heartless shrug

He had a keen, intelligent mind composed of cold logic

It was as if her emotions were nothing to him

Her tears were met by his sigh of annoyance

He had a ruthless reputation, even among the rest of his kind

He had a reputation as a vicious, unforgiving man

He acted cold, detached, as if these people were beneath him

Her words were no more meaningful to him than the chattering of birds

Even after all they'd shared, she clearly meant nothing to him

He sighed and looked away, making her feel like a fool

He huffed and folded his arms over his chest

There was no openness to him, no wedge to access his heart

He was closed to new ideas and opportunities

His interest in her seemed confined to business only

If he cared for her at all, he gave no sign

The billionaire ran his empire with emotionless efficiency

He ran his love life like his business—with cool, distant efficiency

AMBITION AND GREED

He was young and ambitious, with an eye for conquest

Overweening pride and ambition were the ruin of many a man

His ambition would be his downfall

Confidence was one thing, but ego was something else

His ego got in the way of every decision he ever made

There was nothing he would not destroy to feed his ego

Once he knew what we had, he was determined to take it

No cost was too great to achieve his goals

Ambition drove his every waking moment

Ambition guided him to seek out his dream

He was determined to be the best

His wealth was his primary concern

His business was his only concern

Ambition blinded him to the plan's danger

Now was not the time for ego, but cooperation

He was a fool not to question her flattery

She was haughty and prideful

She was far too sure of herself

She aspired to claw her way to the top

Her ambition was to control him utterly

She made men her puppets

She had a ruthless, predatory mind

They underestimated her skills, but not her ambition

She was determined not to let her past hold her back

The man was well-known for greed

His greed had made paupers of us all

His greed devoured all in its path

His greed was a hungry thing

He would not rest until he made his fortune

He regarded our land and its people with greedy eyes

Given half a chance, he would pick us clean

He rubbed his hands together, chortling at his newest acquisition

There was nothing he would not steal

He was a thief and a liar, but somehow charming

Soon, her nimble fingers had pried the object loose from his pocket

Greed had been her undoing

She could not rest until she made the man hers

Her greed forced her to take more and more risks

Greed was her only lover

The only god she bowed to was greed

Her slim hands caressed the object possessively

Dislike and Disgust

He scowled at her

He grimaced in distaste

She frowned in thought

She frowned with displeasure

She frowned, unsure how to answer

He frowned, unsure how to go on

He had nothing but contempt and disdain for her

His scorn grated on her last nerve

It was obvious he'd rather be anywhere but here

She disliked him immediately

The man's boorish behavior disgusted her

She turned away in disgust

The violence repulsed her

She looked away, sick at the sight of him

A gruesome feeling of regret washed over him

The horror was too much and she turned away

Pale and feverish, she turned away in disgust

He averted his eyes and leaned against the wall

Embarrassment, Shame, and Surprise

He was well aware of the effect he was having on her

She fought back a blush before answering him

She felt a hot blush settle over her cheeks

A flush of shameful red spread over her cheeks

The bitter flower of shame bloomed across her cheeks

Her face heated

She turned pink

The pink flush deepened

She reddened in embarrassment

She put a hand over her mouth as if she could take the words back

Shame colored her pale cheeks

Color spread across her cheeks

She blushed, hating herself for loving his words

Shame weighed her down

She had acted shamelessly and now paid the price

She knew only sin, shame, shock

Her mouth moved, but remained soundless with shame

Shame choked her

His mouth dropped open at the sight of her

Complete surprise was etched on his face

He was more than surprised, he was stunned

She stared at him, speechless

Her mouth dropped open in a hushed "O" of surprise

Her voice rose in a shrill of surprise

The shocking joy sent her swooning

Surprise drained the blood from her face

She jumped at the sound of the sinister voice

A soft gasp of surprise escaped her

Shock and surprise rendered her speechless

Words failed him

Fear and Shock

His gaze burned with such intensity she felt her soul shiver

Nerves fluttered in her belly

The fear was writ large on his unshaven face

His eyes bulged in fright

Ice shivered down his spine

Cold terror gripped her in its icy embrace

A cold worm of fear gnawed at her spine

Icy tendrils robbed him of action, freezing him in place

He could do nothing but watch, paralyzed with fright

The fear ate away at his sanity, reducing him to a gibbering wreck

It was more than fright, it was a freezing of the soul

Haunted by horror, all she could do was watch helplessly

She dare not do anything for fear of making the wrong decision

He knew one wrong move would cost them their lives

She did not know what to do and so sealed her fate

She felt an agony of despair

Fear knotted inside her

Her body couldn't curl tight enough to stop the fear

The cold light of fear shone in her eyes

The thought of it tore at her insides

A wave of apprehension washed over her

— Romance Writing Rules —

The romance genre is bound by several important rules:

- The romance between your couple *must* be the main plot.
- Your couple must meet (but not necessarily fall in love or even like each other) by the end of the first chapter.
- Show your couple in a variety of situations *and* emotions.
- Never keep your couple apart for more than 3 to 10 pages.
- Force your couple to confront and resolve unpleasant truths about themselves and their relationship.
- There are only two ways a romance story can end:
  - HEA ("Happily Ever After"); or
  - HFN ("Happy for Now")

One last rule: When writing paranormal romance, romantic suspense, etc., be aware that the romance must still take up *at least* 50% of the story. Any less and it no longer qualifies as a romance and will only upset readers expecting one.

His heart hammered in his chest

Frightened beyond measure, she ran

Her fear escalated and reason fled

The fear was raw on her face

Her breath caught in her throat

With slowly mounting terror, she realized what he had done

Her relief was short-lived

Soon, the fear returned

She felt impaled by fear, unable to move

The fear choked the scream from her throat

Overcome by fright, she fainted

Nerves rubbed raw, she screamed in terror

His coldness frightened her

Her eyes were frantic headlights of fear

She was torn between anticipation and dread

The fear was eating her alive

A haze of fear clouded her judgment

Terror shone from her eyes like twin candles of fright

Terror came gasping up her throat in a cold, panting fear

The fear strangled any chance of escape

She fought her fear and lost

Twisted fingers of fear clawed his guts

He was scared, but had to act or all was lost

Fear gave her courage—the courage to see it never happened again

Even faith was no refuge from that awful fear

The raw emotion came spilling out of her in a terrified moan

Eyes wild with fear, her lips desperately called my name

The frantic fear pulsed like a living thing between them

The fear beat in him even louder than his heart

The cold knot of knowing clenched tight

Fear rendered him powerless against the enemy

And in that terrible silence, the fear grew

The fear was a living thing inside her now

Enslaved by fear, all she could was submit

His was a surrender born of fear, not honor

The toxin of terror blazed through his veins

She was trembling, and he had to snap at her to break the trance

Fear stretched like a shadow in the alley of her mind

Startled faces turned, staring at him in fright

Fear flashed through her mind

Her gut knotted at the thought of losing him

In a flash of fear, she realized too late what was happening

She choked on fear like a fist down her throat

Terror numbed her

Terror slowed her reflexes

The terrible truth was too much

She recoiled in panic from the grisly scene

A pall of dread hung over her, numbing her to inaction

He instantly became wide awake

The shocking truth slammed into her full force

Her wide eyes looked at him in alarm

She glanced up, startled by the strange noise

His body stiffened in shock

The shock left him uncertain how to proceed

The shock was too much for her soul to bear

She felt faint, feverish

She collapsed in a dead faint

Her heart nearly stopped at the shock

One look at that ghastly scene and she swooned to the ground

She felt faint, feverish

She collapsed in a dead faint

The shock of it sent her swooning

Utterly repulsed, she let the faint sweep her away from that awful scene

HAPPINESS AND FLIRTATION

Happiness filled her

Joy overwhelmed her

She was complete at last

Everything was perfect now

Everything had turned out better than she had planned

To have such a man, on such a day, filled her with joy

She relaxed into a state of warm bliss

She smiled at the thought of him

Her spirits lifted at his touch

She approached the task with her typical cheerfulness

He gave her a cocky masculine grin

He gave her a wink and a grin

His smile was lazy, like a Sunday afternoon

His smile was lazy and loving

His smile was pure male

He had the confident smile of a man used to getting his way

The corners of his mouth turned up

An amused smile played across his lips

The smile slid across his lips easily

She coaxed first a smile, then a grin as he relaxed

Her smile was comforting

Her grin was playful, inviting

She gave him a playful smirk

She flashed him a knowing smile

Her lips curved in secret knowing

HATE AND REVENGE

Her eyes grew hot with hate

His eyes bulged with hate

Hate came off him in waves

His voice became ice, cold and sharp as a scalpel

A black curtain of hate fell over his graveyard eyes

He had given into his hate and there was no turning back

The hatred gnawed at him

He lived for nothing more but to kill those he hated

His hatred made him blind

Hate was an ugly thing, and on her, doubly so

The fires of hell stoked the hate in his heart

Only hate lived behind those hell-hot eyes

He let go of his hate only at the moment he died

He carried his hate into death and beyond

Brutal hate and bloody ruin blazed behind those bloodshot eyes

His cruel mouth twisted with hate

His knuckles knotted with hate

His blood boiled with the foulness of hate

Every word was contempt, every look hate

The cruelty of his hatred knew no bounds

Day by day, the anger ate at her, nibbling her nerves raw

The fierceness of his hate blazed like a oven

Childhood hurts cooked in the juices of his hate

She nursed her hatred like a child

She nursed her hatred like a wound

His hate was an open wound only love could heal

The hatred festered in his thoughts

His hate was a cancer on her life

Those who survived her hate never crossed her again

He released his hatred in a torrent of death

Without his hate, he was nothing

He ate hate the way other men eat breakfast

Her hateful eyes clawed at his heart

She promised through clenched teeth and sudden anger

With mounting rage, he turned on her

His hostile glare was hard as daggers

He choked back anger

The hate was in his voice now, hard and cruel

His voice grew cold, harsh and stony with years of hate

Contempt spilled out of her like an open wound

His contempt shocked her into silence

Spit sprayed and hate flew from his mouth

He raged an endless torrent of abuse at the man

Fists clenched in fury, he stalked forward

The cauldron of her eyes burned with scalding fury

Hate beamed from his eyes like hit-and-run headlights

The old king gloomed and glowered at us from his throne

Hate hardened her heart to his pleas of innocence

Anger burned hell-hot in his gaze

Her heart held grudges her lips dared not speak

Eyes blazing, she slapped his face

His angry voice stabbed the air

His voice cracked hate like a whip

His cruel face twisted in anger

The raw fire of hate blazed in her voice

The wrath was upon him

It was foolish to confront him in this mood

His temper flared and fierce words were spoken

He leveled his icy gaze on her and smiled—but not with his eyes

The smile never touched his eyes

His smile was cold and cruel, just like him

Her chill smile was never touched by the warmth of love

He fed on hate and it festered inside him

The cancer of hate gnawed on his last nerve

Soon, he must explode

And all the while, the hate-bomb ticked inside him, waiting to go off

His fake smile disturbed me because I knew he had always hated me

Her bitter words burned like arson in his veins

Her hate boiled over in a shrill, punishing tone

Her hands became claws that raked for my face

A storm of sinister emotion rolled across the stranger's face

His anger damned him, yet he could not stop

The cruel flower of hate bloomed in her heart

His hate, the old killing rage, gripped him

A terrible hatred spilled over him and ate at his guts

He hated himself, but projected that hate outward, blaming others

He couldn't stop killing until they were all dead

She hated him and burned for revenge

He would find a way to make them pay—in blood

Purple with rage, he vowed revenge

Humiliated and betrayed, her hate turned to poison in her mind

To make them suffer was the sweetest wine

Betrayal was the worst crime of all, and one that must be punished

The fires of revenge kept him warm through the darkness

His vengeance was swift and terrible

His vengeance revealed the depths of his hate

His vow was their death

His hate burned on, even after death, so that others took up his cause

She went about her revenge with a singleminded tenacity

The icy road of revenge led her to the slopes of madness

Now, revenge was the only thing left and he reveled in its white-hot fury

Her tortured brain screamed with shrill cries of revenge

Blood demanded blood, and her revenge would be swift

Her heart leapt at the chance to avenge

Vengeance was his lover, hate his only emotion

A wave of hate spilled from the killer—hate and righteous fury

His revenge was her undoing

His vengeance hit home and no one was safe

His eyes bulged with hate and the desire for revenge

Hate guided the avenger's hand

With one last thrust of the blade, his revenge was complete

His heart was black with vengeance

Without the possibility of revenge, her mind sank into despair

Revenge would come, swift and sure

She wanted to hurt him, make him pay

The power of hate drove him like a mighty engine of darkness

The raw wound of her heart demanded revenge

His hatred warred within him

Hatred burnt her bitter soul black

JEALOUSY

The jealous snake of envy hissed in her heart

The cruel worm of jealousy burrowed into her

He wanted all they had and was determined to get it

Jealousy, naked and cruel, gnawed at her thoughts

In a jealous green rage, she cursed him and all men

Her jealous nature forbid her from forming close attachments

She had to have everything first or better than her friends

Everything he said or did was misinterpreted by her jealousy

Her jealous heart hungered to possess him, body and soul

If he could not have her, no one could, and the knife would prove it

Jealous and possessive, he was cruel in his affections

He regarded her with insecure, suspicious eyes

The jealousy had driven her mad and there was nothing he could say

She just *knew* he was seeing someone else

LOVE AND ROMANCE

They became lovers by night and dreamers by day

He was her every hope and fantasy

She saw her heart reflected in his tender gaze

He kissed her tears away, filling her with new happiness

For the first time in her life she felt attractive

With him, she felt truly wanted, desired

She leaned against his chest with a sigh of contentment

He was such a beautiful man, and he was all hers

He wondered whether he could see into her soul

He found himself drawn to her

He was more approachable than most men

He never pretended to be anything more than what he was

His heart slammed at the sight of her

Her heart thudded in her chest

Her heart pounded at his nearness

Her heart throbbed, her pulse raced

Her pulse quickened whenever he was around

He laughed, delighted with her

Her laugh was husky and open

He had a need to touch her, to take all her hurt away

He couldn't remember a time when he hadn't loved her

Only she could bring warmth to his cold, dead heart

Her love was bringing him back to life in ways he had never imagined

They belonged together, and she was determined to prove it

She accepted his faults the way he accepted hers

Theirs was an easygoing kind of love, uncomplicated by silly drama

He wasn't a poetic man, but he made her understand he loved her

Everything good in his world was lying in bed with her

She was a part of everything good in his world

She was his whole world, and he devoted himself to her

He was soft, gentle, and tender with her

She loved how tender he was

She couldn't believe how giving he was, how open

She wanted to share everything with him

Her body, mind, and soul were his, treasured keepsakes of her trust

She had freely given her love and he had given his

They were perfectly matched

Maybe their match wasn't perfect, but it was damn close

She had never fallen in love so easily, or so completely

She devoted herself to him, and he to her

Her true beauty was her perfect soul

He had loved her at first sight, without shame and without regret

She made him feel he could do anything and he loved her for it

Her gentle encouragement had worked wonders on his confidence

The quiet passion of years simmered between them

A wedding seemed the next logical step

She could scarcely believe she was his bride

She had never seen a more handsome groom

To take him to husband would be the ultimate accomplishment

With him, she felt safe, protected, adored

There was no other man for her

No other man was so perfect, so well-matched

She felt safe nestled in the protective cage of his arms

She loved being the focus of his attention

He cherished her completely

If tonight was all they had, they would make the most of it

He was intense and deeply passionate

She'd thought she needed space and time, but she only needed him

His heart beat for her and no other

SADNESS AND DESPAIR

Only despair dwelled in the smoking ruins of my soul

Hot tears of shame slid down her rose-colored cheeks

Blinded by tears, the grieving girl ran from him

She gulped back sorrow her eyes could not hide

Sobbing, she begged for forgiveness

Tears fell like rain from her troubled eyes

Tears welled in the bottomless blue pools of her eyes

Her face grew pale and withdrawn at the mention of his name

She bit her lip in dismay at his approach

She bit back tears of grief

No holiday cheer could warm the winter cold from his heart

She wore her sorrow like a shroud

The aching sorrow soured him like an old wound on a rainy day

Overwhelmed by sadness, she collapsed into the chair

The color drained out of her face

The misery finally broke through her fragile control

The sorrow she felt—the guilt—was almost too much to bear

Her throat closed in grief, she could not breathe

Hot tears welled behind her eyes

Desperate tears spilled down her cheeks

With a defeated heart, she put her face in her hands and wept

She was trapped without hope

Anguish stabbed her like a knife

His cruel words hit her like bullets

Miserable and alone, she faced the sad truth of her situation

The inner torment was all too visible on her bitter face

He gave a resigned shrug as they led him away

Despair twisted and turned inside her

The torment of his decision kept him up at night

Her heart ached with the loss of her friend

Her dress was somber, her face sunless

Her face was ashen with grief

Her voice was thick with sorrow

The open wound of her soul cried out for relief

The dismal weather did nothing to warm his spirits

A gray light of gloom cast its deathless shadow over her

Sadness weighed heavily on her like a stone she carried on her back

All color bleached from her cheeks

She felt the pain sweeping inside her

Loneliness hit her, striking her broken heart like lightning

A crushing wave of despair drowned her

Why do so many writers create cardboard heroes and wimpy lovers? It turns out writing a "real man" is harder than it looks! This fascinating **quick-start guide** will teach you the **top 5 secrets** of how men think and feel and *why*. It's an eye-opening, one-of-a-kind toolkit for today's busy author!

eBook and Trade Paperback available now

— PART 2 —
Bodies & Souls

— Romance & Erotica —

Afterglow/Waking Up

She cleaned herself with a towel

She cleaned his cock with her tongue

He was still semi-hard as he lay panting beside her

Afterwards, her legs were like jelly

He folded his arms behind his head, watching her sleep

He woke spent, pleasured, and alone

Her body pulled away as if burned

She tried to extricate herself from his slumbering embrace

He rolled off her, spent shaft still twitching

He collapsed into the tangle of her slender limbs

He fell back, panting

She was surprised to see she had not milked every drop from him

She threw open a window to let the night air cool her skin

She lay with him, relishing their connection

He leaned back, breathing hard

The quickie had left her a rumpled mess

Hard loving had become heavy breathing in the afterglow

She found peace in his arms

She leaned back with pleasure-glazed eyes

He had made her his woman

She had made him her man

She marveled at the power she had over him now

The bedroom was one of the few places she could control a man

They dozed, wrapped together in the blissful afterglow

They lay quietly panting in the aftermath

Her body felt deliciously sore

She settled into his embrace

She rubbed him clean with a washcloth

She cleaned herself, then curled up beside him

She raised her head to look into his sleepy blue eyes

Exhausted, she fell asleep in his arms

His half-lidded eyes slid closed as he breathed her name

She woke tangled in the sheets

Her body was sprawled limply on his

She rested her head on his shoulder

She enjoyed being held

He gathered her against him

She savored the nearness of him

She turned her face into the pillow and dreamt of him

They lay curled together, in each other's arms

She lay on his chest with her head tucked under his chin

She woke slowly, languidly, remembering the night before

She let her body relax into his, a sigh of contentment on her lips

She nestled against him under the covers

She turned sleepily onto her back

A rustling sound made her open her eyes

He lay propped against the pillows, watching her

She woke to his kiss

An urgent kiss woke her

She opened her eyes to find him between her legs

He woke to a warm female body next to his

She woke to warm sunlight and a world made new again

She woke to strong male fingers between her thighs

She woke to possessive male hands on her breasts

She woke to his mouth on hers

She woke to a kiss that tasted of last night and all the nights to come

Arousal, Lust, and Temptation

Lust burned in his brain and he could think of nothing else

His fingers yearned to touch her, his mouth to taste her

He had to know what secrets hid inside that soft, yielding flesh

Forbidden flesh was the sweetest of all

A lusty feeling of warmth stole over her

His eyes caressed her with lusting, invisible fingers

Almost against her will, she began to undress for him

Shame and desire mingled hot in her throat

He had a strange kind of animal magnetism that drew her to him

She was disturbed by the raw power of her attraction to him

She was powerless to resist his foreign charm

Blood throbbed in her veins with a scarlet web of desire

He was all she wanted, all she could think about

His pulse quickened with forbidden longing

The glow of desire became a bonfire of lust that consumed them both

A delicious shudder shot through her body at the thought of him

Every inch of her lit up with the burning, urgent need to possess him

Pleasure pulsed in her veins

She worried his soft words were spoken in lust, not love

Theirs was a mutual attraction, and a mutual destruction

What they shared was not love, it was madness

He made her hunger

She thrilled to the thought of him moving inside her

Her body went warm at the thought of him

Raw, wild need passed between them

They were love's hungry savages, primitive in their desire

There was only this last night of mad lovemaking

Their lovemaking was intense, stoked by carnal ferocity

They became nothing more than hunger, need, love

Theirs was a desperate dance of the flesh

They were joined together by more than flesh, but by their souls

They had become creatures of the flesh

Their bodies had become slaves to biological need

Urgent with need, she drew him to her

He had an animal's hunger

Raw need met pure desire

Animal hunger took over

The flame of desire kindled between her thighs

She would tame this male with her body

She wanted him in her mouth

She wanted him inside her

His pounding need to be inside her was too much

Her overwhelming need for him blotted out all reason

He sent the old familiar shiver coursing through her

She was a slave to the new sensation, willing to do anything for more

Raw need had made him brutal with desire

Theirs was a savage lust, an animal mingling

She was mad with lust, mad for him and all his body offered

His lust for her was timeless and potent

She drove him wild with distraction

She wanted to claim every male inch of him

He was all-man—hot, hard, and exquisite

She teased him with the promise of her body

She smiled her sultry come-on smile

Heat uncurled in her abdomen

Heat settled in his groin

Her lust was an emotional hunger that could not be denied

He was mad for her, mad with desire and animal longing

She was hungry for the forbidden

Her carnal desires could no longer be denied

She obeyed only her lust now, and consequences be damned

There was fire in her loins and desire in her belly

That she wanted him inside her she had no doubt

Warmth swirled through her belly at the thought of him

A powerful force passed between them, a wild, sexual heat

She wanted his hands on her

She wanted to touch him, taste him

She went hot—hot for him, hot for this moment

The ache between her thighs grew more and more insistent

The fury of desire trembled within him

She allowed herself to appreciate his beauty

He exhibited a raw sensuality

She knew she should run from him

She had glimpsed the danger simmering under his cool facade

There was a danger about him that drew her in

She saw he was all man, inside and out

He drew near, close enough to kiss if she dared

His sheer maleness overwhelmed her

Every instinct she had said he was different

His nearness seemed to invite her into his embrace

His masculine energy dominated her

She angled her knees toward him as he talked

Her interest in him continued to heighten

She wanted to give in to his need, and to hers

She wet her lips with her tongue

To tempt him was dangerous

He was obviously at home in his sexuality

She was wild, open, and willing

He wanted to crush her body against his

The attraction was mutual

Desire raced through his veins at the sight of her

Anticipation pulsed through him

With pouting lips, she teased him

There was something about her that made his blood go hot

She set fire to him, arousing every sense, every thought

She hungered at the sight of him

She fought a shiver of arousal

Her pulse raced, palms dampening at the sight of him

He wanted nothing more than to indulge in her pretty flesh

All he could do was fantasize about being with her

He had enough fantasies about her to fill a hard drive

She trembled between desire and fear

Wet heat flared between her legs

Hot cream coated her opening

Her body betrayed her, wanting him

She went slick and hot

Her body spilled out a wet welcome at the sight of him

She felt herself go all slippery inside

She knew then she needed him wild, pounding inside

She imagined each thrust, every shared pleasure

All she could think about was touching him

She thought of him and touched herself

He felt himself harden at her memory

He was so hard he hurt

He took himself in hand, fantasizing about her

He imagined her lying naked and brazen before him

He needed her body under his

He wanted to see her squirm and writhe under him

Terrible hunger crawled through her, the kind that could eat a man

Lust made her go mindless, insatiable with craving

All reason fled, leaving only the madness of desire

She didn't need gentle, didn't want it

Only rough pleasure would sate her now

She was torn between unease and arousal

He was hard and hungry with need

BED

They stumbled like drunks into bed

She stared at their nude bodies reflected in the mirrored ceiling

She was laid out on the mattress waiting for him

She leaned back against the soft pillows, daring him to join her

She patted the mattress, inviting him to come to bed

She lay on her side, one breast soft against the sheet

The headboard rattled

His hands fisted around the headboard for support

With each thrust, the headboard slammed the wall

The bed trembled beneath them

The bed creaked

The bed groaned, but not nearly so loud as she

The bed collapsed, spilling them to the floor

They tumbled out of bed

The center of the bed was soaked in their juices

He rolled over onto the wet spot and cursed

Body and Face Descriptions (Female)

Her beauty was intoxicating, a balm on his wounded soul

She had curves more dangerous than any mountain road

Flickering candles gave her skin a soft satin glow

Her body was warm and soft

Her skin was satin soft

Her skin had the allure of satin

He traced the delicate lines of her tattoo

Her skin was flawless, sensual, and made for loving

She was woman-soft, all curves and candy to his male mind

Her curves were more than a match for any man

Her curves bent and trapped his mind

His mind traveled south along her curves

Her slim body was tanned and toned from years of aerobics

Beyond flexible, she moved in ways only a Yoga student could master

He couldn't stop staring at her magnificent face, her perfect body

She had sun-kissed skin

She had an hourglass figure

Years of corset-wearing had nipped in her waist

She was voluptuous beyond belief

She was petite, a mere wisp of woman

There was a fierceness about the way she was built, a terrible attraction

Her full figure was well-cushioned, pillowed for pleasure

She was a big, beautiful goddess of desire

She was built to drive men wild

She was all flowing flesh and hungry curves

She was round in all the right places

She had soft skin, but there was muscle under it

She was fit and toned with a light dusting of freckles

She had an elegant, swan-like throat

She was boldly unashamed as she swayed toward him

She bounced and swayed, delicious jiggles that caught his lustful eye

Her gorgeous body made him ache with need

Her swelling curves held the creamy power to entice and compel

She had a Gothic quality, like the doomed heroines of old

She had a Mediterranean beauty

She had the olive skin and dark hair of a Greek goddess

Her skin was pale gold

Her skin was honey gold, her body petite and playful

Her skin was perfect brown, her body flawless

Bright eyes glittered from that dark and lovely face

Body and Face Descriptions (Male)

He was chiseled perfection, a storybook prince

He was all sleek muscle and untamed pride

He was gleaming skin and rippling muscle

His body was thick with muscle

He had the hard, muscled body of (a warrior, an athlete, etc.)

He had the lean, wiry physique of a (thief, dancer, etc.)

His body radiated a raw and primal strength

He had a sleek, powerful build

He was a beautiful man

He had an intelligent face and charm to match

She admired the planes and contours of his chest, arms, and shoulders

He was lean and sinewy

He had long, sensitive fingers—artist's hands

Inked bands looped around his bulging arms

He had a full sleeve tattooing him from wrist to shoulder

His tattooed back was covered in soaring lines

He had scars from the war

He had rough, calloused hands, the hands of a construction worker

His thighs were keenly muscled like the rest of him

He had the strong calves of an athlete, powerful, but not too thick

This man was like a fantasy come to life

He was a magnificent, naked god

She sighed at his sheer, gorgeous perfection

He had a square jaw and high cheekbones

He had sharp, hawk-like features that radiated intelligence

His face was predatory, primal, but not without compassion

A storm of emotion briefly passed behind his normally impassive face

His body was a solid wall against her, impassive, unyielding

His heavy male body body pinned her

His weight settled over her

Body Heat

He covered her trembling body with his own

They were skin to skin

The length of his body burned hers with a shared and searing passion

His body heat seeped into hers

His body branded itself on her

She wriggled against him for warmth

She shivered and pressed herself against him

Her body molded against his

She melted against him

She felt the rough heat of his hands on her

His hands were hot, demanding more and more from her

Fire raced from his body to hers

The shared heat and sensation thrilled her

Their heat warmed them through the long winter night

Heat met heat, a shared inferno to warm them through the night

Bondage and Kink

With the mask on, she was blind to all but pleasure

The blindfold only added to the fun

She wondered what he was doing and shivered in anticipation

To know those big strong hands were touching her was beyond erotic

She strained to hear any sound, any little clue

She was blind, without eyes but not without pleasure

The blindfold had ridden up just enough for her to peek out

When the blindfold came off, she gasped in surprise

The ropes held her in place, naked and vulnerable

The ropes bit into her wrists

The ropes were silk, but his will was steel

She eagerly obeyed his every command

— How to Divorce Yourself from Weak Writing —

Here are three easy exercises designed to divorce you from the bad habit of lazy descriptions. Pick a category or subcategory of tags that you know will be important to your story, especially a subject you feel you're weak on (such as "Vampires" if you're writing a paranormal romance).

Exercise #1: Read all the listed tags from your category or subcategory, making note of the top ten tags you like and the bottom ten you don't. Now challenge yourself to revise, combine, or otherwise alter all ten of your favorite tags, then do the same to improve your least favorite ones.

Exercise #2: Combine parts of tags from one category with those from another, mixing-and-matching as best you can to create new effects. For example, a tag from "Breasts" could be combined with one from "Touch."

Exercise #3: Challenge yourself to come up with at least ten totally original tags on your favorite subject. Dig deep, and feel the gates of inspiration open!

He made her beg for it

He teased and tormented her, pushing to the brink, then pulling back

She braced herself as the whip cracked

The lash burned into her

The cat o' nine tails *thwacked* against her

The loss of control, the total surrender, was deliciously new to her

She yelped as hot wax dripped onto her skin

He demanded her complete submission

All she had to do was obey

He made her crawl to him

She behaved according to his will

She was obedient, compliant

He was always in control

She got a sick thrill from being his slave

She wanted him to wreck her

She wanted to be totally destroyed by his pleasure

She wanted him to split her in two

He denied her pleasure until she gave in to his demands

With each stroke of the lash, something in her shattered

She bowed her head in delicious submission

The shaky excitement of her submission was electric

Her body belonged to him now

She was his perfect pet, a willing disciple to depravity

She writhed for him, senseless and submissive

He was tender in his cruelty

He kept her bound to the bed

Her hands were bound as if in prayer

He made her sleep in a cage at the foot of his bed

She hung by her wrists from a hook in the ceiling

He handcuffed her to the bed

He lashed her to the bed posts with silk rope

He cuffed her hands behind her back

He cuffed her to the bedpost

He bound her body: hands, breasts, crotch, feet

The ropes bit into her soft flesh

Her brain emptied of all thought but the desire to serve

Giving up control built such terrifying excitement in her

His fingers owned her, his mouth, his cock too

She wanted him to overpower her, to force her to submit

She felt branded by him, owned

He taught and trained her in the forbidden ways of pleasure

His strange, forbidden love had left its mark on her body and mind

His lust had become a devouring obsession

She was his to possess, body and soul

She had become his plaything, his most prized possession

It was impossible to do anything but obey his every command

She lived to obey, to worship and adore him completely

The billionaire bound her squirming body

She loved the feel of the ropes on her

His games turned darkly erotic, almost dangerous

BREASTS

She dragged the blanket up to cover her breasts

She used one arm to cover her breasts

She covered her breasts instinctively

She blushed and covered her exposed breasts

Her bosom heaved

He watched the gentle rise and fall of her bosom

His eyes settled on her breasts, so perfect and proud

Her breasts were round and full

Her breasts were perfect handfuls

Her breasts were ripe, succulent mouthfuls

Her glorious mounds were catnip to male desire

Her breasts bounced with each savage thrust

The round swell of her breasts tempted him

Her breasts thrust invitingly toward his mouth

Her breasts heaved against him

He cupped the heavy underside of her sweet mounds

He felt the sweet weight of her breasts pillow against him

Her perfect breasts bobbed and swayed

He nuzzled her breasts, savagely licking and sucking at the tips

He cupped her breasts in his hands

He squeezed and caressed her breasts, gently at first, then rougher

The heavy weight of her breasts pressed into his face

She teased her nipples across his chest

Her nipples hardened against his chest

Her nipples rose, diamond-hard and full of desire

Her nipples tightened to sharp peaks

Her nipples went tight

Her already hard nipples tightened further

Her nipples were ripe berries waiting to be plucked

The stiff nipples left no doubt she was aroused

He teased the hard buds of her nipples

He tweaked her nipples

He returned his attention to her breasts

Her breasts were half-covered by her bra

Her breasts spilled eagerly out of her dress

She exposed the creamy swell of her breasts

Her breasts felt swollen, the place between her legs damp

Her breasts were ripe handfuls to his hungry hands

His thumb and forefinger teased the taut bud her exposed nipple

He caught each nipple between thumbs and forefingers

His hands closed over her breasts, trapping them

Her nipples ached where they pressed against the fabric of her dress

She pulled her neckline down so her breasts popped into his hands

Hard nipples strained against the fabric, nipples waiting to be free

Her nipples became hard pebbles pressing against the fabric

He felt the shape and softness of her breasts through her dress

He felt her nipples grow hard between his fingers

His fingers found the hard point of her nipple

Strong hands curved over her ribs, covering her breasts

She thrust her breasts more tightly into his hands

His hands cushioned and massaged her breasts

His hands tightened on her breasts

He rolled and pinched her nipples

His thumb rasped against her hardened nipple

Her breasts were lush, rose-tipped and teasing

Her breasts quivered against him

Her breasts smashed against his hairy chest

He splayed his fingers across the sensitive mounds, kneading them

Her breasts shifted in a delicious bob

She deliberately rubbed her breasts against him

Her breasts filled his palms

He squeezed and kneaded her breasts

He fondled her breasts

He kissed his way to the valley between her breasts

He molded and shaped her breasts, stroking the nipples with his thumb

Her nipples were dark, hard buds crying out for his tongue

Her nipples were a dusky rose

Her dusky nipples responded to his teasing touch

Her breasts ached with need

Her nipples grew hard, becoming almost painful to his touch

Her breasts swayed and bounced with each teasing step

He took her left nipple in his mouth through the fabric

He lapped at her nipple, working the tip to life

He flicked the sensitive tips of her nipples with his tongue

His tongue flicked over the hard peaks of her nipples

His mouth closed over her one nipple, his fingers working the other

He paused to suckle first at one nipple, then the other

His mouth moved to her neglected nipple

He sucks her nipple deep in his mouth

He took her nipples between tongue and teeth, hardening them

He lingered on the gentle swells of her breasts

He covered the nipple with his mouth, suckling her

His mouth tugged at her sensitive nipple

The honeyed flesh of her breasts welcomed him

His cock slipped between her huge mounds

He slid his shaft in and out of the valley of her cleavage

He kissed his way up the slope of her breast

He took a breast in each hand

Her breasts bobbed on the water's surface

Breathing

Her breath came in soft pants

His breath whispered over her lips

His breath was a hot caress

Their breath mixed hotly

He inhaled her

His breath grew ragged as she had her way with him

His breath was ragged in her ear

Her breath hissed, a sound that was half-pain, half-pleasure

She gasped with each measured thrust

She gasped for release

She sucked in air

Their breaths mingled in intimate confession

A sharp gasp escaped her lips as the sensation built

Breath panting, bodies fusing, they knew this was right

Her breath hitched

He blew warm air over her nipples

His breath touched her throat

BUTTOCKS

Her sweet bottom swayed for him

His hands gripped her ass, pulling her close

His hands closed over her bare ass

He clasped her behind

He gripped the ample flesh of her ass

Her ass was round and full

He palmed her ass

His large hands cupped her ass cheeks

He gave her butt cheeks a hard squeeze

His hands smoothed over her generous ass

Her broad derriere was like a magnet to him

His hands cupped her generous backside

He gripped her ass, squeezing, caressing

His hands squeeze her butt so hard she cries out

She squirmed and wiggled her plump bottom

She thrust her behind at him, daring him to take her

The cleave of her buttocks beckoned him

She knelt on all fours, begging him to ride her

She rolled over and raised her ass

Her soft cheeks quivered and trembled at his touch

She twerked and worked him

She crawled on hands and knees, ass wiggling

He smacked her butt, sending a shivery thrill up her spine

He slapped her ass to watch it ripple

He pressed intimately against her backside

He ground his erection against her backside

He spanked her beautiful plump ass

She felt the hot slap of his hand on her ass

Her bottom bore his handprints he had spanked her so hard

She was red-bottomed and sore, but regretted nothing

She grabbed his butt and pulled him closer

Carrying

He lifted her from the bed

He lifted her in his bronzed arms, carrying her to the wedding bed

He caught her by the waist and carried her to bed

He swept her into his arms and carried her to bed

He swung her into his arms and carried her upstairs to bed

He scooped her up and carried her to the bed chamber

He whisked her into his arms then brought her to bed

He settled her on the bed gently

He threw her into bed and was atop her in an instant

Clothes (Removal)

She undressed with efficiency

She shrugged out of her jeans

She stepped out of her shorts

Her gown fell away, revealing the naked glory of her flesh

Her gown slithered to the floor

He eased her dress off

He tugged her skirt from her hips

She raised her skirt

She lifted her skirt

She stripped off her dress

He shoved her jeans to her thighs

His hands parted her clothes

He tore her dress off

He wrenched her skirt up

He pulled her nightgown up and snugged himself in behind her

He unzipped the back of her dress

He ripped her T-shirt off

He tugged the straps of her bra to her elbows

Her bra came off

He fiddled with the front hook of her bra

She unclasped her bra

He fumbled with her bra

He tugged down the cup of her bra

He'd barely had time to see her fancy silk panties

She kicked off her boots

She stepped out of her heels

Her clothes came off, layer by layer

Everything came off except her pointy-toed heels and stockings

One by one, her garments fell until she stood naked before him

He unlaced her corset with slow hands and deliberate desire

He unbuttoned her blouse

Hands shaking with need, she stripped for him

She unbuttoned her frock

His hand pushed aside her skirt

He dragged her panties down, that last lacy barrier to his lust

He removed her soaked panties

He tore the thong off

In an instant, her panties were gone, torn off by male hands

He pushed aside her panties, impatient with need

He ran his fingers along the edge of her panties

Her bra and panties went flying

Her fingers tugged at the zipper

Her trembling hands went to his zipper

She unzipped his fly

She pulled his zipper down, eager to tame the taut serpent inside

She tugged his zipper down and reached for the prize inside

His abs clenched as she ripped open his jeans

Hungry fingers slid in past his denim

His hardness sprang mercifully free from the prison of his jeans

The head of his erection strained against the soft cotton of his briefs

He toed off his boots

He pushed down his jeans and underwear

She stared hungrily at the bulge growing in his pants

She worked at his trousers, trying to free the beast inside

She tore his shirt off, buttons and all

She twisted her hands into his shirt

His belt rasped off, buckle clinking as it hit the floor

He whipped off his shirt and approached her, bare-chested

EYES

Her eyes were blind with desire

Her eyes fluttered shut

Her eyes glittered in the firelight

Lights flashed behind her closed eyelids

Her eyes clouded in a sexual haze

Stars flickered in the corner of her vision

The world dimmed around the edges

His gaze was mad with lust, with molten desire

Her pupils were fathomless, filled with desire

His eyes were clamped shut, his mouth open

A raging beast of need was in his eyes

His eyes turned dark with desire

She batted her eyelashes

Her bright-colored eyes met his

His direct gaze unsettled her

He watched her with an intent look

He watched her curiously

He gave her body a bold, sweeping gaze

There was a hint of fire in those eyes

His eyes flicked to her cleavage

Her gaze followed the sleek lines of his arm

Bold eyes raked her soft skin, promising pleasure

He held her with his eyes

She had big, trusting eyes with thick black lashes

She blinked, eyes hot with desire

She winked at him lasciviously

She looked at him helplessly through tear-tipped lashes

Her pupils were dilated, dark with desire

He stared deeply into her eyes

Her gaze dropped to his jeans

She stared at his growing bulge, knowing it was her doing

Desire flared in his eyes

His bold eyes raked her

His heated gaze was on her

She met the heat of his gaze with her own

Her dark, almond eyes had an inquisitive look

His eyes were full of heat

Pure sex was in his eyes, pure need and desire

His eyes went hard and distant, impassive to her suffering

A fan of black lashes flickered over her cheeks

Slowly, she opened her eyes

Foreplay (Female on Male)

She wrapped one slender hand around his erection

He grew even harder in her hands

Her hands were close to his crotch

She was anxious to taste him, to take him into her mouth

She was amazed at his thickness

His hardness rubbed against her

His cock grew to life in her practiced hand

His cock grew, filling her hand, and didn't stop there

His cock grew, straining toward her, aching for release

She gripped the base of his cock and lowered her head

She pulled him to her, his arousal pressing her belly

He stroked himself to hardness

His shaft strained upward in a thick curve

The blunt head of his erection pressed urgently against her palm

She made a fist around his shaft and began to move it back and forth

She pumped the hard flesh, urging it to action

She slid her hand up and down the length of him

A little fluid leaked from the tip and she used it to lubricate the shaft

His cock came alive in her hands

He was rock-hard and ready

He was hard with arousal, hard for her and only her

Her slim fingers circled his erection, feeling its urgent heat

His cock was a magic, growing thing she yearned to have inside her

His cock grew thicker, harder, and longer than she'd ever imagined

Her fingers closed over his hard flesh

She felt his organ swell

His swollen organ was hers to command

She held him and knew her power

Her strong fingers stroked him

His shaft jerked and jumped in her hand

His erection was hard, yet soft, like him

Her hand moved over him faster

Her hand moved in steady rhythm designed to drive him wild

She took his arousal in one skillful hand, working him into a frenzy

Her lips moved toward his erection

She took him into her mouth

Her mouth worshipped at his altar, taking him in with devout desire

She charmed his supple serpent with her tongue

It was as if her mouth was meant to hold him

He slid his tautness into her mouth

Her mouth was a trap of moist heat for his manhood

She flattened her tongue under the sensitive tip

Her tongue glided over his shaft in rasping strokes

She reached for the button at the top of his fly

She dipped her head to taste him

She licked him like a cat

She lingered on the tip

He loved her mouth on him, craved it like a drug

He was male candy to her and she licked and sucked at his length

She moved her head up and down the hard length of his erection

His body bucked as she worked his shaft

His fingers knotted in her hair, working her head up and down his shaft

She took his hot, thrusting cock into her mouth

She sucked hard at his swollen member

She used her tongue to stroke the underside of his shaft

His cock was so big she nearly choked on it

She forced her throat to open wider for him, taking him deeper

She deep-throated him, her mouth a hot, wet oven for his release

Her mouth sucked him, desperate for the white juice waiting inside

She watched his face as she sucked him, loving the reaction

She traced the thick veins with her tongue

She led him by his erection toward the bed

FOREPLAY (MALE ON FEMALE)

She was eager for him to explore her

He nuzzled the inside of her thigh

His hand reached for the apex of her thighs

His hand reached for that most womanly and secret part of her

His fingers stroked her, sending her into shivers of ecstasy

One hand touched the damp curls that gathered around her cleft

He found her slippery, throbbing nub and worked it

He slid his fingers inside her

Her thighs clenched around his head

His clever tongue set off a blinding heat inside her

He explored her with his tongue

He was drowning in her taste

His tongue lashed inside her, working her open, driving her wild

The lash of his tongue kept her prisoner to desire

His tongue tantalized and teased her

His tongue teased her open, questing, conquering

She lost herself in stroking, licking, petting

He stroked and petted her

His hand slid between her legs

He worked his strong fingers into her, igniting her

She writhed against his hand, lost to pleasure

His fingers touched flesh no man had touched before

His caressing fingers made her ache for him

His swirling fingers spread her wide

His thumb sank into ready wetness

He pushed a second finger into her

His fingers moved over the soft tuft of hair

He ran his hand over the vee of dark hair

She grew embarrassingly damp at his touch

Her sheath grew slippery at his touch

The dark curls between her legs glistened with her juices

Moisture beaded and dripped between her legs

His thumbs parted the wet folds of her labia

He curved his fingers to stroke her deep and slow

He rubbed her sweet berry

He teased the hard nub of her clit

His tongue circled her drenched bud

Her clit cried out for him

He teased and worked her folds

She arched into him as he ate her

He drank deep from her candied well of pleasure

He sheathed his tongue in her

His mouth never stopped working her wet center

His tongue found her trigger and fired off short little licks and sucks

The bold swipe of his tongue sent her spinning into pleasure's arms

Hair

He clenched his hand in her hair

He wove his fingers though her hair

She entwined her fingers through his hair

Her fingers delved into his hair

Her fingers tunneled in his hair

She brushed hair out of her face and kissed him

She pushed her hair away

He brushed her hair away

His fist bunched in her hair

His fingers speared into her hair

He touched her hair, smiling at its beauty

Her long hair fanned over the pillow

She swept the braid back over her shoulder

She undid the braid, letting her hair fall over her shoulders

Her hair fell, loose and lustrous

Her hair tumbled over his chest

She had a glossy mane

Her hair was silk

Her hair was fine-spun silk, luxurious to the touch

She had silky curls

Her hair had been bound into an unforgiving bun

Her hair was piled high in the fashion of the day

She had cut her hair short

She had a short bob

She had a pageboy cut

She had short, spiky hair

Her hair was a living work of art

His fingers moved through the blond glory of her hair

Her hair was like a golden halo

Firelight danced in her hair

Her hair was a violent splash of color against her pale face

The dancing flames made a halo of her hair

Her hair was a blaze of copper

Her red hair was a smooth cascade of fire

Her hair was night-dark

Her hair was shadow black, inky in the moonlight

Her hair was raven-black, a shimmer of midnight

She teased her long hair over his chest

Her hair was soft between his fingers

She laced her fingers through his hair

He buried his nose in her hair and breathed her in

Her hands tangled in his hair, clasping him closer

Her hair tickled his hips and thighs

He liked the way her hair slid over his skin

Her hair had a rich, lustrous sheen

Her hair had been newly done

She had bound her hair in a loose ponytail

She let her rain down

Her hair was the perfect frame for her heart-shaped face

Her hair spilled across the pillow

Her curls tickled his chin

She tossed her curls over one slim shoulder

The little hairs on her arms raised

The hairs on the back of her neck raised

His chest was lightly covered in soft, golden hair

His chest hair tickled her breasts

His hands were snarled in her hair, controlling her

She shook her hair back, wild and free

She pushed back a wisp of hair from her eyes

He had the long, flowing hair of a swashbuckler

LIPS AND KISSES

He brushed his lips to hersdar

Her lips were plump and red

She touched his lips with a playful finger

His fingers traced the delicate softness of her lower lip

He lifted her up into his arms

She tucked her head under his chin

She trembled in his arms

His love could ease the hurt

He nuzzled her neck

His mouth was on hers, telling her without words she was loved

It was a kiss to end all kisses

He cupped her head and kissed her lips

She loved to hear his sweet words

His mouth was tender, his embrace sure

He kissed away all doubt and fear

His fingertip traced the outline of her lips

He lifted her up and carried her across the threshold

Their kiss was long and leisurely

His lips were warm and welcoming

His mouth swooped in to steal a kiss

He took her lips with his own

His kisses were cruel, devouring her will to resist

They kissed open-mouthed, panting as their bodies worked

Their lips met in a wet, hot slide

He broke the kiss and bit her lower lip

He gave her lower lip a hungry nibble

His mouth moved down her slender throat

She kissed her way across an expanse of bare skin

His lips worked hers

His mustache tickled her where he kissed

Her lips were swollen from kissing his stubbled cheeks

The kiss was hard, then soft, then hard again

He swept into her with an earth-shattering kiss

They kissed and pounded and tore at each other

The sharp need of her kiss aroused him

His kiss set off a sharp, wild need in her

It was a brazen kiss that held nothing back

She pressed a kiss to his palm

Their kiss was wild with passion

They shared and slurped at his each other's mouths

His kisses were slow, wet, and coaxing

A kiss like this could only have one conclusion

The kiss was bone-tingling

His blistering kiss set fire to her soul

He swallowed her helpless cry with his kiss

She ravaged his mouth with kisses

He ravished her body with kiss after kiss

She teased his lips with a kiss

He hit her with a kiss that set fire to her heart

He trailed kisses down her cheek

Her mouth opened to his kiss

He lowered his mouth to hers

This was a kiss at full burn, a firestorm of passion

His lips were petal soft, brushing her mouth, then moving lower

His kisses began softly, then built in intensity

His kisses pushed all else from her mind

She lifted up on her toes to reach his lips

She pressed her lips more firmly to his

He took control of the kiss, cradling her head in his hands

The kiss was possessive, greedy for more

He claimed her mouth with a savage kiss

His lips crushed against her

His clever lips pressed to hers in an unspoken promise

Where his lips touched, her body came alive

He dropped a kiss upon her belly

She was consumed by his kisses

Her kisses were hot, wet with desire

He deepened the kiss

He pulled her close, kissing the nape of her neck

He could kiss her forever

She lost count of his kisses

His kisses were tender, yet with the heat of male power

He kissed her again and again

Each kiss made the world go away

To kiss her forever would never be long enough

She captured his lips, kissing, sucking, nibbling

He kissed her fingertips

His kiss was coaxing, confident

He poured everything he had into the kiss

Each kiss sent licks of electricity through her veins

He angled her mouth for a deeper kiss

The kiss was more than satisfying

The kiss had been a long time coming, and everything she hoped for

His merciless mouth rained hungry kisses upon her

And still the kiss went on, unbroken, eternal

It was a drunken kiss, but a kiss all the same

She rose up to kiss him

They kissed rough and deep

She moistened her lips with her tongue

She pressed a kiss to his forehead

He kissed his way up her throat

Her lips settled on his mouth

He kissed her smooth, rosy cheek

His slow, sensual lips were on hers

He kissed her slowly, with an intensity that was dreamlike and erotic

He kissed like a lover and there was nothing chaste about it

These were no longer flirting kisses, but hot, demanding ones

Her lips were lush and red

His lips were eminently kissable

Her plump lips pillowed his

His kiss crashed into her heart

He landed a punishing kiss on her mouth

He silenced her protest with a kiss

He kissed her pulse, pleased by her arousal

There were so many ways to kiss him

His lips were gentle, kind, loving

His kiss was hotly tender

It was an impossible kiss, born from shared madness

When they kissed, it was fireworks, champagne, and so much more

The kiss lingered long after his lips left

Mouths, Teeth, and Tongues

He adored her mouth with his tongue

She opened her mouth to him

His mouth ravished hers

His tongue warred with hers, invading her mouth with a wet heat

Their tongues fought a silent battle in the warm cave of her mouth

He nuzzled his way up her to playfully bite her earlobe

His mouth was on her neck, breathy and hot between kisses

They bit and sucked and tasted each other in the velvet darkness

She placed his fingers in her mouth, teasing them along her tongue

Their mouths mated, teeth and tongues savage with desire

She nibbled on his hot skin, working her way down

He tasted her mouth for the first time

Their tongues slicked together

His mouth worked its magic on her

Her teeth raked his neck

His teeth scraped her shoulder

His teasing mouth came close, begging to be kissed

She felt his mouth, his hunger

They tasted each other deeply

His tongue slid inside her mouth

It was as if her mouth was meant to hold two tongues

She liked the feel of his tongue rubbing hers

She sucked on his tongue

His tongue filled her mouth

She pressed her mouth to his

His tongue tickled her belly button

She sucked and nibbled at his neck

His foraging tongue pushed past her lips

Their tongues entwined

Their tongues tangled

Their mouths were alive with wet heat

Theirt mouths met, tongues probing, tasting desire

She darted her tongue between his lips

Hungry lips rained hot kisses fueled by forbidden desire

Their savage tongues circled like two snakes saying hello

The kiss was eager, the taste sweet on her tongue

Before he could finish the sentence, she covered his mouth with hers

His mouth possessed hers

His mouth trailed along her collarbone to the hollow of her throat

His mouth slanted over hers

His probing tongue demanded a response

He nibbled her ear

He lowered his mouth to her throat

His mouth wandered from hers, tracing the contour of her throat

His mouth covered hers, wanting her sighs, taking them

Her mouth was perfect, ripe, and willing

Her mouth was made for kissing

His tongue captured the dark recesses of her mouth

His tongue conquered her mouth

Her mouth was moist and feminine, her breath sweet

Her heated, passionate mouth savored him

She moistened her lower lip with her tongue

He licked his way down her neck

He tasted her tears

He tasted salty tears

He licked her tears away

His talented mouth sent shivers down her spine

His clever tongue did new things to her

His teeth scraped over soft skin

His tongue rimmed her ear

Her mouth went dry with dusty pleasure

He had a man's mouth and a man's desire

His mouth commanded hers to obey

He felt the tiny prick of her teeth

She nibbled and sucked, leaving a love bite

He sucked her toes, massaging her feet

She bit down in his shoulder

His mouth never left hers

ORGASM AND PLEASURE (FEMALE)

This was the ultimate pleasure

Her whole body was on fire with pleasure

She luxuriated in the sweet sensation

Her entire body vibrated in response

Her body gave a surprised jerk, then melted into him

Her body was awash with overlapping waves of pleasure

Her body bowed to sensation

Her toes curled and back arched as she came

Her toe-curling orgasm left her shattered on the sheets

Pleasure shot through her at his touch

He felt the pleasure ripple through her

The sensation sizzled through every part of her

The rough motion sent her over the edge

She teetered on the brink, then fell into impossible pleasure

Convulsive waves gripped her

At the peak of her orgasm, she was like a madwoman, shrieking passion

Her orgasm crested like an ocean wave

Sensation ripped through her, a tumbling wave

Her teeth clenched and toes curled

She came in cascading waves

Pleasure rocketed through her

Her orgasm hit full force

His gifted mouth brought her to climax

A soul-shattering orgasm robbed her of her senses

A bone-tingling orgasm reverberated through every part of her

The orgasm scorched her body clean

The building shivers consumed her

The tension inside her exploded

Her body was shaking, brain reeling

She gave into the moment with total surrender

He was working her into a frenzy

Heart pounding, body quivering, she saw stars and felt fire

Her senses shattered as she came

Powerful sensations built and throbbed below her waist

Thrills ran up and down her body

Every nerve ending quivered

She came with soul-wrenching satisfaction

Through the long winter night, they pleasured each other

With burning bodies and molten hearts, they became one

She came in quivering waves

Heat streaked through her

She squirmed against him

Her body clenched around him

She grabbed his hair and pulled him close

Her frantic hands gripped his shoulders as she came

A white-hot climax ripped through her

She writhed against him, hot and wild

Every inch of her body was alive with savage energy

She was riding a near-painful edge

She was close, so desperately close to release

Her body went taut, every secret part of her crying out his name

When she came, it was an explosion of pleasure

Her body was torn by pleasure

Her body was gripped by a pleasure she had never known

She screamed in release, legs clenching, body convulsing

Pleasure and release stormed through her

Liquid fire streamed through her body

Her body, long in pursuit of pleasure, had now found sweet release

Her muscles spasmed around his cock

Overwhelmed by passion, she gave in to her release

She came on his tongue

She thrashed against him

Her entire body shuddered, head tilting back in soundless ecstasy

Her silken sheath clenched around his hot steel

Liquid fire singed her veins in a scorching wave

Multiple orgasms tore through her

The pleasure would fade, then build again

Her body spasmed around him, lost in the throes of pleasure

Mindless ecstasy gripped her as the orgasms rippled through her

A wild orgasm ripped through her, then another

Tension coiled inside her, then released in a white-hot wave

A greedy orgasm gripped her, making her body its slave

When she came, her orgasm was intense

Her body crippled with pleasure, intense and insane

Her body gave into the scandalous pleasure that gripped it

She was dizzy with desire, with the feeling that pulsed between her legs

Blissful, blistering pleasure seized her

Her mind splintered, shrinking into primitive passion

She felt herself erupt and then there was no more thinking

Pleasure short-circuited her brain

She became lightning and shooting stars, a love-streaked comet

A shock of pleasure possessed her

A raw, rippling wave washed over her from breasts to thighs

Molten desire pooled in her core, then erupted in cataclysmic waves

The orgasm washed her mind clean of reason, leaving only raw need

She thrashed and moaned, lost in her climax

The orgasm stripped her of her usual control

The buzz of sexual heat built between her legs—built, then burst

Energy burned between her hips, riding low on her spine

Pleasure tore her in two

The force of the orgasm shook her

The climax shook her, made her a helpless rag doll of desire

Her body writhes in orgasm overload

Erotic oblivion grips her, sends her screaming over the edge

She felt her bones go liquid, her soul shivering in contentment

Her orgasm was a blade that severed her from all reality

ORGASM AND PLEASURE (MALE)

She coaxed him toward his climax

He fought his own release

He forced himself to slow down

He pulled back on his mental reins, mind desperate to control his body

He strained body and mind, fighting the rush that built within him

He gritted his teeth against the oncoming sensation

He was fighting the sensation, struggling to hold on just a little longer

The need to explode built in him, a rising crescendo

He moved hard and fast, jackhammering toward a desperate climax

His pulsing cock raced to climax

He clasped her hips, pulling her hard into his final thrust

He pounded home, bursting into her and filling her with his seed

His pulsing cock gushed into her

He felt his balls tighten in response

The sweet suction of her mouth was too much

She cradled his balls as he came

He cried out in pure pleasure

He came with a growl

He came in a rush of hot cream

He growled with pleasure

She sucked him to orgasm

She swallowed his spurting come

He came with a shuddering cry

She licked up every last pearly drop

She tasted his salty come

Hot seed coated her belly as he pulled free

He poured his seed inside her

He burst in a bone-deep growl of pleasure

He coated her in his love

His seed shot in a hot arc

His storm of lust blew inside her

He blew into her like hurricane

He blew into her with the force of a storm

He thundered into her like a storm

He shot his seed into her, her body milking him of every last drop

The hot spray of his seed was like lightning inside her

He unleashed his love into her

Hot love erupted from him, virile and volcanic

No woman had ever felt so good, so perfect

He melted in her heat

His body tensed, blood pumping hot

He spilled himself into her

He exploded, a hot blast of male coating her core

He flooded her

Hot come splattered the sheets

He spilled hot seed on her breasts and belly

He came in salty, lava-like spurts

His eruption was violent and virile, leaving him gasping

His manhood danced and sprayed, coating her in hot sticky love

White juice squirted in her liquid heat

He stayed inside, letting her body milk him

He grunted from the pure animal satisfaction of his release

His released his warmth into her with a savage grunt

He bucked and moaned, then poured himself into her

He thrust deeper, faster, then went absolutely still

He was paralyzed by pleasure

Every muscle tensed as he came

His release was hot and violent, savage like him

His breath rumbled as he neared—then crossed—the point of release

He stiffened and convulsed, a roar of satisfaction upon his lips

His body jerked hard, every muscle tight as he poured himself into her

A fireball of pure bliss raged inside him

Orgasm and Pleasure (Mutual)

They climaxed together

Fueled to new heights, they came as one

All she knew was her release, and his

They bucked and thrashed against each other in shared release

When the climax came, it came for them both

Theirs was a shared pleasure, perfectly giving, perfectly taking

When they came, it was with the heat of the sun

Their bodies shuddered, blasted by bombs of pleasure

They gasped and groaned, giving into mutual pleasure

They came hard, each fueling the other's climax

They were pure heat and pleasure

Friction on friction, they pummeled each other to the edge

Passion burst where they were joined

Their bodies fused in one shared hot, sticky release

The power of their orgasms sent them into shivering ecstasy

They came together in shuddering waves

They came in mutual surrender

Penetration

She spread her thighs to receive him

The junction of her thighs was ready for him

He pushed her knees up and wedged himself between her thighs

He parted her thighs

Her opening throbbed for him

She was wet and ready, begging for it

His shaft teased her entrance, rubbing without entering

He teased her folds, coating himself in her wetness

His erection slid across the damp curls between her legs

He pushed his heavy erection against her opening

He briefly paused at her pearly gates, then pushed them wide

The silky heat between her thighs captured him

Her legs opened wide to receive him

Emboldened by her own reckless desire, she guided him in

She was bold, insistent, guiding him into her most intimate place

His length pressed against her front, hard steel ready for her forge

His rigid shaft stoked the furnace of her loins

He moved himself against her, teasing her folds open

His erection filled her, stripping away everything but her need

They moved together as one

He lifted her up and onto his throbbing cock

He pressed her into the wall even as he pressed himself into her

He pushed himself into the heated core of her body

His knees were inside her thighs, spreading her open

He thrust into her, the tendons on his neck standing out in sharp relief

She rotated her hips in slow circles around his cock

He pulled out almost all the way, then plunged deep

He pressed harder into her, deeper, filling her up with his maleness

She met his driving rhythm beat for beat

Arching her hips, she met him thrust for thrust

She moved under him, moaning as he filled her

His cock seared into her, burning like a brand

He plunged into wet heat, a scalding hotness that gripped him

Their bodies joined as one

They had joined their flesh in that age-old animal dance

She was deliciously tight

At first she thought he was too big

He was impossibly huge, and hurt so good

Her pussy tightened around his shaft, milking him

She straddled him, easing herself down, taking him in

Her passage quaked and trembled at his entry

His hugeness seemed to stretch and devour her

He filled her completely

He began to move inside her

His length speared her

His girth stretched her

She stretched and melted around him

He rode her woman's body with the passion of the beast

Faces close, fingers entwined, they moved to the raw rhythm

She straddled him, hips grinding

She drew him into the dark heat of her passion

He parted her delicate folds with one bold stroke

Her damp heat stroked him, held him prisoner to her charms

He rammed himself home, his body hard and primal against her

She locked her legs around him, holding him captive to her lust

He rode her, using her hair as reins

Hard, rough strokes rocked her body

She lifted her hips to meet his strokes

Fingers locked, eyes locked, they became prisoners of desire

He slid into her with blunt promise

She was stretched, filled by his manhood

She felt him at the tip of her entrance

Slowly, he slid into her

Her silken glove squeezed down, trapping him inside

Her muscles gripped him tighter

His relentless thrusts rammed into her

He rolled her onto her back and eased her thighs open

He was her mighty prince, her stallion, and she rode him hard

She rode him as well as any stallion

The thick head of his cock lodged inside her

Deep, steady strokes shook her

She couldn't believe how wide he was

She couldn't believe he actually fit inside her

And now that hugeness was inside

He was filling her, stretching her wider than he thought possible

He drove into her with an animal fierceness

He took her with pounding need and driving hunger

Hearts beating, bodies melding, they moved as one

She sheathed him, marveling at the perfect fit of their flesh

She gasped at how he filled her better, more fully than any other man

The tension built between her legs until she had to have him inside her

He planted himself inside her like a tree sinking its roots into the earth

The pulsing root of his manhood surged into her

Her petals parted easily for his surging cock

She rode his shaft, taking him into her, taking all of him

Her velvet prison caged that most animal part of him, making it hers

Her body welcomed him

Her wetness received him

Her hips rose to meet him

He lost himself in her wet warmth

She was wet, she was wild, she was his

The welcoming suction was more than any mouth could give

Hunger matched hunger as their bodies came together

Body to body, mouth to mouth, they moved

Their merging bodies collided

He penetrated deeply, burrowing toward her molten core

He sank his aching shaft in her wet heat

Her flesh closed around his shaft, hugging him in the ultimate embrace

Hips bucking, shaft throbbing, he plundered into her

She was surprised at how her body sucked him in, holding him tight

She thrust her hips, gyrating, grinding atop him

He thrust into her from behind, clasping her hips hard against him

She lowered herself onto him

He stretched her to the limit

Her inner walls rippled against him

The lean beauty of his hips thrashed against her

He groaned and pulled out a little, then drove back in

He opened her with his fingers, then teased the tip in

His strokes were slow, sure, and possessive

Each hard thrust sent her reeling

Pleasure racked her body with each firm thrust

He pistoned harder, his shaft slicking in and out

Her damp entrance swallowed him in one swift plunge

She was trapped between torment ecstasy

Her body ached, demanding more, begging to be filled completely

He hammered into her, a hot rush of pure need

He slammed into her, rough and gasping

He thrust and stroked, thrust and stroked

The fury of his deep thrusts filled her

She enjoyed every single second of holding this man inside her

His cock was ruthless, plowing into her, driving deep

Her muscles stretched to accommodate him

Delicious friction penetrated every nerve

Her body held him in a vise-like grip

Her sheath gripped him

She held him tight inside

Her pussy clenched and rippled around him

Her body trapped him, a soft fury of womanly need

Her weight was on him, pinning him inside

She bore down on him, her desperate straddle taking him deeper

Their lower bodies entwined

She twined her legs around his waist as he rode her

She met his strokes eagerly, fueled by her own passion

She was a hellcat under him, all wet, wild fury

— Superlatives for Lovers —

Need a quick list of ways to describe your couple's most endearing qualities? Here you go:

adventurous, amazing, athletic, awesome, beautiful, becoming, bold, brash, brave, brazen, breathtaking, caring, charming, clever, compassionate, cute, daring, dreamy/dream-like, easygoing, erotic, exotic, exquisite, fantastic, fabulous, fetching, fit, flawless, forbidden, generous, gentle, glamorous, goodhearted, gorgeous, handsome, healthy, heroic, honest, hot, incredible, intelligent, invincible, loving, lovely, loyal, muscular, noble, out of this world, passionate, perfect, rugged, rough, seductive, shameless, skilled, strong, talented, tender, toned, tough, true, undeniable, unstoppable, untamed, virile, warm, wild, wise

His fingers rubbed her as he thrust in and out

She worked her clit as he pounded into her

He invaded her, setting fire to her passion

Penetration (First Time)

Pain lanced through her

Pain stabbed at her, replacing the pleasure of moments ago

She knew pain then, aching, stretching, tearing

She gasped at the invading thickness that suddenly filled her

This was no wagging tongue or finger, this was *him* inside her now

She looked down and saw herself impaled on his shaft

She gazed down and saw their bodies were joined

He had taken her by surprise, spoiling her pleasure

With one nightmare thrust, he was inside

He slammed past her maidenhead

He thrust inside her virgin opening

He pushed another inch in, then paused and pushed again

She was tighter than any fist

She was so tight, it was almost painful to work his way inside

She felt no more than a pinch, then it was done

She told him to wait a moment, not to go any deeper

He eased himself out of her, then slid back in slowly

There was surprisingly little pain past the initial shock

There was a pinch, no more than a moment's pain

Soon, pleasure returned, and she sighed in relief

She was unprepared for the painful pleasure

She winced and whimpered at first, then began to enjoy it

He stroked in and out, taking her for a ride unlike any other

She felt stretched and hot and no longer a girl but a woman

And in that moment, she became a woman

She felt what became the beginning of pleasure

He had taught her what a woman could feel

At first, she had been content to lie there, but now she moved eagerly

He had taken her innocence and given pleasure in return

He pulled out, surprised to see dried blood on his shaft

There was dried blood on the wedding sheets, proof of her virginity

Pregnancy

She wanted his seed in her, wanted it to grow, flourish, and bind them

He had planted his seed, and this was the result

He placed a hand on the slight bulge of her belly

He pressed a gentle hand to her bump

He laid a possessive hand against the fertile swell of her belly

He kissed and licked her swollen belly

He couldn't believe how big she was getting

The passion in her grew more swiftly than any child

Her one-night stand threatened to become a lifetime commitment

One night of pleasure, and she'd be paying for it the rest of her life

She glowed with health and new life

She had the fresh, healthy glow of an expectant mother

Protection

She tore the condom wrapper open with her teeth

She rolled the rubber slowly down the length of him

He removed a condom from his wallet

She tore open a box of condoms

She reached for the condom wrapper

He plucked a condom from his pocket

She slipped the condom's ring on over the head of his cock

They put the condom on together

The condom sheathed him, but could not contain his passion

His blunt tip strained against the condom

He was so thick, she could barely fit the condom on him

She worried he would get her with child, but not enough to stop

She should have stopped, but the pleasure was too much

She gave a brief thought to using protection, then was lost to passion

He pulled out, but not in time

Scents

He breathed in the scent of her

The scent of her was intoxicating

Her body smelled of flowers and soft summer days

The floral notes of her perfume hung in the air

Her perfume was doing things to him, things he could not resist

Her perfume permeated the jungle night

Even doused in perfume, her need filled his nose

He could smell the woman under the perfume

Her musk bloomed like a flower at his touch

There was no hiding the musk of her arousal

He could smell her arousal

She smelled like heaven

She smelled of woman and raw, untamed nights

The sex-musk was strong on him

He had that earthy, male scent that drove her wild

His wild male scent aroused her

He had a clean, dangerous scent

She drew his masculine scent into her nose

She had a particular fragrance that reminded him of his youth

His scent ignited a wild heat in her

The fireman smelled of smoke and desire

He smelled of cigarettes and whiskey

She could smell the alcohol on him

He smelled of the woods

He smelled secret and earthy, like the forest at night

The clean scent of fresh pine clung to him

The manly spice of his cologne filled her nose

She smelled his spicy aftershave

Sounds (Female)

She moaned at the mouthwatering view of him

She moaned his name

She whispered for more

She whispered his name

She begged for more

She made a begging sound

She made a frustrated sound

She gave a breathy little moan

She gasped and pulled away

A hum of satisfaction slips from her lips

She leans back, humming in satisfaction

Desire was thick on her tongue as she begged him to come to her

Her tormented groan begged him to continue

He covered her mouth with his to swallow every whimper

With a pleasured cry, she found the release she needed

Tortured moans squeezed past her lips

She moaned deep in her throat

She bit back a whimper

The sound she made fed his hunger

Her last word became a moan as he pushed himself inside her

Her voice was heavy with sexual heat

She pressed closer, moaning

She made the soft hiss of a woman: half-pleasure, half-pain

She made a soft sound full of need

She purred, cat-like, in his ear

She purred like a cat

She made a low, throaty sound of pleasure

She groaned against his mouth

A scream of pleasure tore from her lips

She gave a soft gasp of surprise

She moaned, gasped, and writhed, wild under him

She sighed in unashamed pleasure

Her feminine cries excited him

With every whisper, every moan, she made herself his

Her breath came in jagged gasps now

She came with a pleasured cry that shook her to the core

Her mewling keen was loud enough to wake the dead

Her words died, becoming breathy moans instead

A sob of feminine joy burst from her

She squeaked in protest

She gave a hoarse scream of pleasure

She bit back a whimper

SOUNDS (MALE)

He blew a hot breath in her ear, then panted her name

He made hungry sounds in the back of his throat

He let out a rough shout as he came

He came with a hoarse cry

He sighed with satisfaction

He made a smug sound of male pleasure

He made a rough-voiced request

His throat grew thick with desire

His voice husked her name

He sounded feral, brutish in his heat

He made a wholly sensual sound, a low rumble of pleasure

He stifled a hungry groan

His words became passionate grunts

He fell on her with a voracious growl

His words vibrated through her

He spoke in an affectionate whisper

He murmured words of love

Sounds (Mutual)

There were no more words, just sounds of passion

They made sounds without words, noises of pure animal pleasure

They moaned into each other's mouths

The sound of sweat-slick skin slapping filled the room

Together they gasped, moaned, and writhed in the sultry summer heat

They panted pleasure, lost in sexual heat

They made sounds of stark need

They grunted and gasped, locked in a mad embrace

Sweat

Her skin shimmered with perspiration

Her skin glowed with a faint sheen

He licked at her pulse, tasting salt

His skin was slick to the touch

Her body glistened with perspiration

Tiny beads of perspiration covered her body

Her body was damp and gleaming in the firelight

His sweat-dampened body covered hers

Her body was hot and slick in the summer heat

His skin tasted of salt

He tasted her skin

Her salty-sweet flavor drove him wild

He tasted every inch the man, virile and ready to mate

His erection slid across the damp flesh of her thigh

Her hair was plastered against her face

Her damp skin was salt-slick as he ran his tongue over it

His hair was damp and sweat dripped down his face

Pleasure drenched their bodies

Their skin grew salty with shared passion

Sweat made them shimmering outlines in the firelight

Sweat filmed his skin

Sweat dripped from his brow

They were glued to the sheets by their sweat

His masculine torso gleamed with sweat

The damp, dark hairs of his chest tickled her

Touch (Misc.)

She responded to his touch eagerly

Her entire body tingled at his touch

The feel of her skin jolted his senses

He ran his hand up her thigh

She raked her nails down his chest

She clawed at his back

He pulled her forward by gripping her thighs

His body prowled against hers in the dark

She scraped her nails down the hard muscles of his abdomen

She slithered over him, soft, snake-like

He ran his fingernails up her side

His hands slid around her back in a hungry hello

Rough hands squeezed and caressed her buttocks

His hands traced the contours of her body

He caressed her curves

His hand moved to where she ached for him

His body was candy to her hungry hands

She was touch-hungry and would not be denied

His hands felt like brands on her skin

The stubble of his unshaved jaw rasped against her thigh

She let her hands play over his body

He pulled her down until they were nose to nose

He flipped her so she lay beneath him

He cupped her face in his hands

Every touch was a rough promise

Her body softened in welcome to his touch

Her hands roamed eagerly over his muscled male flesh

She pressed her face against his magnificent male chest

He broke the kiss to caress her

His hands were on her waist

She gripped his shoulders

His touch was surprisingly gentle

His hands skimmed along her torso

His hands seemed to sear her flesh

Instinct made her clutch him to her

He touched her and found her body taut with anticipation

She ran her fingers over his broad shoulders

His hand trailed over the curve of her hip and thigh

Her back arched in response to his touch

His arms snaked around her body

His hand against her bare skin sent shivers racing through her

She wiggled against him

He caught her arm and pulled it against his chest

He pinned her wrists to the mattress with a playful grin

She touched raw, masculine skin kissed by the sun

She caressed his well-muscled chest

She felt his power play under her fingers

He petted her thigh

His hand skated down her back

His hands closed over her hips

He knew just how to caress her

He lifted her against the door as she wrapped her legs around his waist

Her hands glided over his arms, testing muscles

Her lush body pressed close

She rubbed gently against him as she passed

She let one hand fall lightly on his arm

She leaned into his touch

His arms were iron bands holding her

His arm swept around her waist

Her body was soft and pliant to his touch

His arms tightened possessively around her

His hands were clamped around her arms, fingers pressing deep

His untamed touch awakened the woman in her

Her sensitive, creamy skin tingled at his touch

Her stomach muscles clenched as his moved over her

She didn't protest his touch

She welcomed his touch

His caress ignited something in her, something she thought long dead

Her curves were his to caress

His body crowded hers, close enough she felt his arousal

One hand slid down her spine

She slipped her hand into his

His touch was electric, his confidence supreme

His hands framed her face

The tip of her nose pressed into his cheek

She could feel the heat of him

His fingers trailed down her belly

Her body whispered like silk against his

Her manicured hands caressed his scruffy chest

His shadowed jaw lay against her chest

She cupped his scruffy jaw in her hands before leaning in for the kiss

He slid a muscled thigh between hers

He was hard everywhere, from muscles to manhood

His work-roughened hands were doing things to drive her crazy

He crawled up her body

His touch stamped his lust into her, his love, his passion, his soul

His hand stroked her ribs, then moved up to her breasts

His hand held her throat

His thumb caressed the soft underside of her jaw

Their foreheads pressed together

His hand was laced firmly in hers

Their linked hands were a gesture of love on public display

He touched her exquisite body as if it were priceless art

He wrapped his arms around her from behind

He snugged her close

His hand was at the small of her back, guiding her

She had petal-soft skin

Her body became a refuge for his roving hands

She buried her face in the curve of his neck

Strong fingers pressed into her tight muscles

The massage pulled the pain from her tired limbs

Her oiled skin became putty in his hands

She kneaded his stiff and aching flesh

His hands felt rough on her skin

He tilts her face up so she can look at him

She felt goosebumps as his touch whispered over her

He traced a line from her belly to her hip

His soapy hand stroked her

His hand tightened on her neck

She drew patterns on his chest with her fingertip

She wound her arms around his neck

His answer was to press her against the wall

The muscles of his abs contracted where her fingers played

She ran slim fingers over his six-pack abs

— *Romance Writing 101* —

Most readers expect and demand that your lovers will meet by the end of the first chapter. They don't have to like each other, and the meeting can be brief, but there should be something about the encounter that clues the reader into the fact that something special just happened. One of them says or does something that sets off an important emotional reaction in the other. This is usually used to illustrate the story's theme (and the main character's problem).

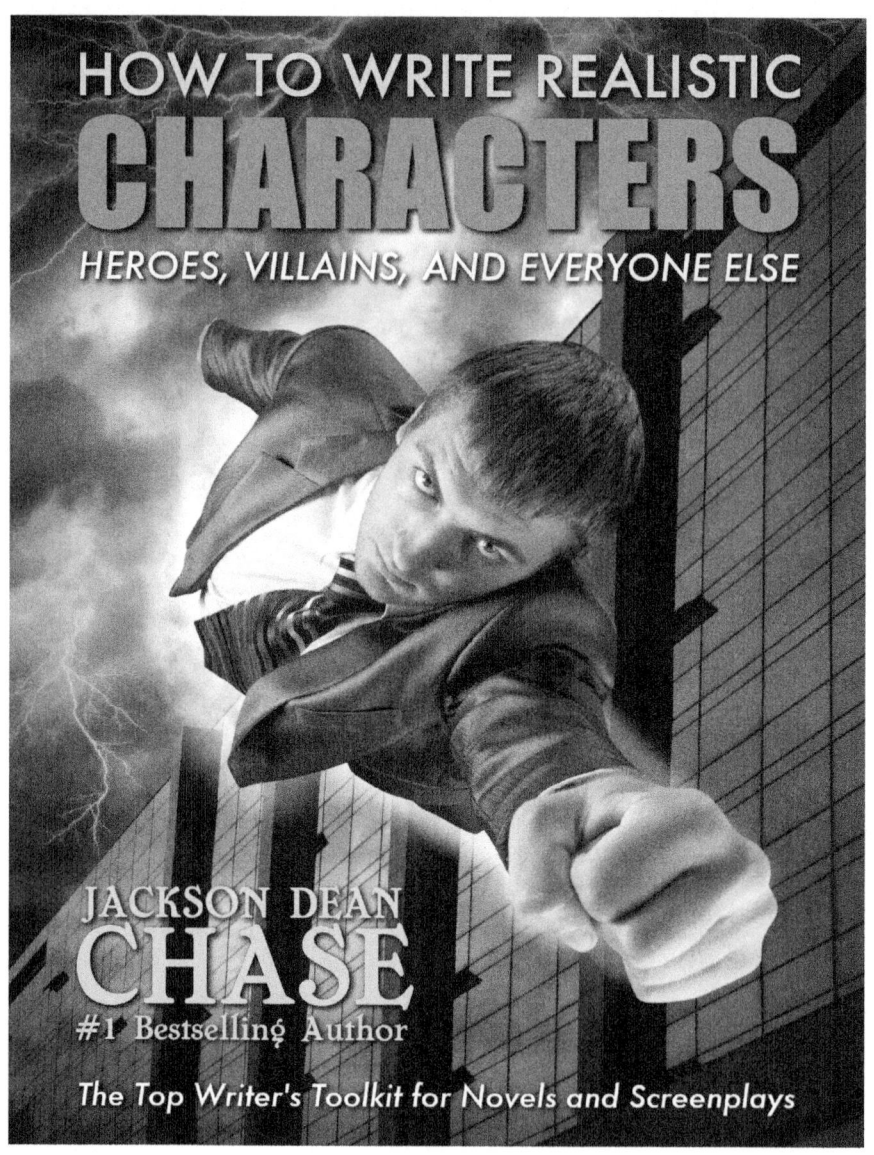

When readers don't believe in your characters, they don't believe in your story. This power-packed book teaches the top secrets you need to know to quickly master writing realistic characters! Best of all, it works with any genre and any format: novels, short stories, series, etc.

eBook and Trade Paperback available now

PART 3
Paranormal & Fantasy Romance

— Supernatural Creatures —

ANGELS

The angel furled its wings

He retracted his wings into his body

The angel spread its wings

His wings were purest white

His wings were singed black at the tips

One wing lay crumpled under him

In a flutter of feathers, the angel was gone

He stepped out her window and spread his wings

The angel flew higher

The angel swept down

He flicked his feathers at her

His sleek feathers fanned her

His head tilted, curious and birdlike

The angel regarded her with rich gold eyes

He had white hair, gold skin, and silver eyes

His quicksilver eyes watched her impassively

The angel drew its flaming sword

The angel sang and the heavens cried

The angel acted without emotion

The angel was cold logic wrapped in flesh

The angel's skin was flawless, hairless, exquisite in its perfection

Its voice was thunder

The angel was perfect, too perfect

Her heart broke to behold a being so perfect

Its true form was pure white light, but it appeared to her as a man

Its aura was warm gold

The clouds broke and the angel appeared

The angel's touch was as soft as its wings

This angel had fallen long ago

The angel had fallen and now walked between good and evil

The angel was made of light and flame

It shone with pure-white god light, impossible to resist

Demons

From within the magic circle, a black mist rose

The magic circle bound the infernal creature

The demon pulsed with nameless power, awakening her desire

He had come from the deepest hell at her command

The demon had a taste for souls

The cunning fiend offered a bargain

The demon granted power to those who dared make a pact

Lesser demons embodied fear and pain

Greater demons embodied tyranny and corruption

The witch's imp mocked us from the shadows

The demon's mocking laughter followed me all my days

Red eyes and crimson claws followed my every move

The demon was greedy for souls, and hers in particular

The bargain was sealed in a banquet of blood and souls

It was a pact no mortal mind could understand, yet I signed it

The demon's true form was sickly black shadow

Demons drew their shapes from their summoner's mind

The demon was an impossible combination of man and beast

The demon's aura was pure evil, malignant and gloating

The demon's aura was pitch black shot through with pulsing red

The succubus took on a more pleasing shape

The succubus preyed on the lustful and unwary

The incubus knew what secrets lay in a woman's heart

The incubus radiated a sinister sensuality that drew women like flies

The demon's forked tongue hissed flattery

The fiends wore flames as cloaks

The demon was quick to anger

The demon was terrible in its wrath

The demon spoke only in lies and half-truths

The demon only spoke true when truth was worse than lies

The demon promised much, but delivered nothing but pain

The demon fed on her tears, drinking them like wine

The hell-spawned horror leapt from the flames, eager to possess her

It possessed her with all the power of hell

The demon refused to be cast out of the girl

The force possessing her was old, evil

Possessed, he levitated before us

My flesh obeyed only the demon now

The demon was bored, hungering for new games

Amused, the demon agreed to her game

The lust demon was red-skinned, sculpted to perfection

The demon had pitch-black wings

He flapped his obsidian feathers in annoyance

He had black and leathery bat wings

The demon bowed its horned head mockingly

Ram's horns curled proudly from his ridged skull

Goat horns curved straight back from his black-haired skull

He had the horns of a bull and a temper to match

The demon flicked its tail in arousal

The head of the demon's spade-shaped tail entered her

He was well-versed in the ways of lust and suffering

He could read her mind and give her what she wanted

Though her magic bound him, his heart remained unchained

Even demons had desires

The demon had never known love, only lust and desire

She gasped as he revealed his true form to her

His unnatural aura dominated her, made her reckless with passion

She needed his unnatural love like a drug

She wanted to possess his body as eagerly as any demon

In that kiss, she saw him for what he was

The ancient power he possessed was nothing compared to her love

Ghosts

The ghost watched her with sad eyes and a lonely smile

An icy chill passed over me as I saw the specter descend the stairs

Clad in white, the weird woman walked the hall like a figure out of time

I knew its love would haunt me forever

Wailing, the ghost lunged and passed right through me

A silvery specter came out of the grave

A low, eerie moan escaped the tomb

In the mirror, I saw another body superimposed over my own

The face in the mirror was no longer mine, but that of a ghost

The ghostly whisper told me to kill

His ghost was all too eager to live through me, in me

The attic grew dark with the spirits of the dead

The spirit danced and shimmered in the dark

Her feet never touched the floor

When he reached for her, he found nothing but air

With mournful eyes, the restless spirit sank through the floor

Gradually, the translucent glow took on human shape

This ghost was no bed sheet and rattling chains, it was real

My will was no longer my own

My ancestor's ghost was in me now, controlling me like a puppet

The banshee's wail brought misery and death

The ghost had possessed the most pleasing host he could find for her

The ghost could not move on until he had secured her love

The ghost entered her with his phantom erection

The ghost became a pleasing vapor that flowed inside her wetness

The ghost came to her in her bed each night, haunting her with its love

Each night the ghost came to her—and came in her

His ectoplasmic seed floated in the air between them

Such a romance was doomed, or so others would have them believe

The bleeding wreck of her soul called to him with nameless longing

His phantom kiss sang in her blood

In death, as in love, the heart ruled all

Her heart knew his and wept for the sorrow of it

The dead had just as much love to give the living

Her haunted face drifted close, promising love

Her heart trembled with longing to be with him

Each night she called to his spirit, the ghostly love in him grew

The whisper of his ghostly lips caressed her

In death, she found new life, new love, and a hope for something better

Desire can be deadly, and many an unnatural love has led to death

Nature Spirits (Faeries, etc.)

The natives said every living creature, every living thing, had a spirit

Nature spirits could be bargained with the same as any ghost or demon

What nature spirits wanted in return for their aid was often confusing

Some nature spirits were as dark and twisted as their homes

Most nature spirits were peaceful until disturbed

The nature spirit had no power outside its home

The nature spirit could not travel far from its home

Within its home, a nature spirit could be incredibly powerful

The nature spirits rode the druidess and she danced, lusty and wild

For a price, the river spirit agreed to help us cross its banks

It was said that the spirit of the pond could steal a woman's reflection

A swarm of pixies covered the intruders in mystic moon-dust

The faeries danced and shimmered as night fell on the forest

The faerie's voice was that of the wind

A faerie's love was fleeting, as fickle as the wind

The mountain faerie's voice was like the grating of rocks

The fire faerie spoke in hisses and crackles

The ice faerie's breath misted when it spoke

The ice faerie shot a volley of icicles and hailstones

The ice faerie conjured a snowstorm that soon became a blizzard

The ice faerie called up a freezing mist to conceal us

The merman spoke in the rising and falling tones of the sea

The merman's kiss was salty and cold, his webbed fingers possessive

The merman's scaly caress conjured up visions of the briny deep

The mermaid sang to the passing sailors

With a flick of her tail, the mermaid disappeared beneath the waves

The dryad was beautiful, elf-like, and serene

The dryad melded into the tree and was gone

The tree-man towered over us, threatening with its branch-like arms

The tree bark twisted, and a man-like face became visible

The unicorn dipped its horned head in greeting

The unicorn whinnied and neighed in response

The satyr clicked his goat hooves in glee

The satyr's pipes played a mad, merry tune

The centaur *clip-clopped* toward her

The centaur was half-man, half-horse, and hung like a god

SHAPE-SHIFTERS (WEREWOLVES, ETC.)

It was a thing that should not be, yet here it was

The were-beast growled, long and low

The werewolf glowered with slavering jaws and murderous mouth

It was a mix of animal and human, embodying the worst of each

Bristly black hair crowned a face so savage, even the dogs fled

Her mouth was a muzzle of yellow fangs and snapping jaws

The two-legged beast lapped hot blood and howled at the moon

The beast man's snout picked up my scent and the chase was on

The beast man's elongated muzzle bared teeth of savage yellow

It was an insane hybrid of man and beast that walked on two legs

The thing was hairy, misshapen, but its eyes held a grim intelligence

The moon was his mistress now

The moon beckoned her to join the pack, to run under the starry night

The chase was only exceeded by the thrill of fangs tearing warm meat

He wore the moon's curse like chains around his heart

The beast was cunning, with the mind of a killer

Every full moon he swore it was the last time

Her skin grew a coat of silken hair

She snapped her teeth at him

He growled, long and low

She shifted back into human form

The fur grew longer and thicker as the moon called her name

The Moon Mother's children were restless to kill

The pack followed the scent of her blood and called for her to join them

Panting, fur against fur, they mated and howled their love

The moon madness was upon them

As he transformed, his mind became small and hungry

There was joy in the gnashing of teeth and tearing of flesh

The pleasures of the hunt soon gave way to the grisly feast

She sank her sharp teeth into his neck, claiming him as her own

The snapping jaws buried themselves in my neck

I felt a rough tongue lapping at my wound

A bloodstained beast watched her from the forest's edge

The first transformation was long and painful

The transformations grew quicker and easier with time

His beastly transformation filled her with awe and dread

He clawed off her clothes, shredding jeans and panties to get at her sex

A single claw cut through the waistband of her panties

He shifted into animal form

The animal in him took over

The beast was in his blood

His mouth sprouted ivory fangs

His beast teeth came out to play

His beast teeth were on her

His teeth closed around her breast, rough tongue working the nipple

His beast teeth nipped playfully

He licked her wound clean

He pinned her to the nearest tree

He wanted to lunge at her, to paw and pant over her naked glory

His careful claws caressed her

He placed his paws on her chest

His rough tongue licked her face, her neck, her breasts, then lower

He was something beautiful and savage

His nostrils flared, scenting her

The smell of her arousal was like a drug to the beast

Night-glow eyes were on her

The pack watched over her while he was gone

The alpha was a predator, prowling the edge of love

The alpha wanted her for his life-mate

Once an alpha mated, it would be for life

His primal hearts was hers

He was volatile, feeling rage and affection often and in equal measure

He was a creature of instinct

His protective instincts took over

He bonded with her, imprinting in a way no man could

He moved with a lethal grace

The beast in him growled

He growled low in his throat

His beast growled with pleasure at her touch

The beast in him snarled a warning

The beast was always prowling just beneath his skin

The beast was in his throat, on the tip of his tongue

His alpha nature demanded obedience

The lure of the moon called her like a lover

The bite healed so quickly, he knew he was cursed

The wolf glowered at me with slavering jaws and murderous mouth

The pack took up the call

Soon not one, but a dozen terrible shapes loped behind me

The awful hunger to kill, to tear and destroy, came upon him now

The fur sprouted on him, thick and musky with the wolf-scent

The whispers of the forest called to him

His voice was half-wolf and all lust

The were-leopard watched me with jealous gold eyes

The were-panther's rippling muscles were midnight in motion

The were-panther was a leaping shadow

Her hand moved over his silky black fur

The were-tiger stalked forward

He moved, cat-like, toward her

In one cat-like move, he was upon her

He pounced and made her his

He purred into her mouth

He purred at her arousal

The were-tiger rasped a throaty, sensual hello

The were-bear was thick-muscled and shaggy

The were-bear bounded through the forest, savage and free

The were-bear carried her back to his cave

Once he saw her, the were-bear lost all interest in hibernating

He wanted to hibernate with her in his arms forever

Her heart swelled like the moon when she saw him transform

His hot breath and soft fur had her panting with desire

He sniffed her with a wolfish grin

With clawed fingers, he pulled her violently to him

Theirs was a dangerous attraction

He needed saving—not only from his curse, but his loneliness

Her love could break his curse as no ancient ritual ever could

Cursed or not, they knew love and it was enough

That she could never truly understand his kind meant nothing

The beast was on her—*in her*—and she became one with it

She could only guess what such a creature could be feeling for her

Her body ached for his fearsome touch

Despite his cruelty, there was something vulnerable about him

He used his claws to shred the T-shirt and bra off her

— *Writing Romantic Heroines and Heroes* —

A heroine never stands idly by letting her lover save her. If she can solve something herself, she should. But that doesn't mean she must do everything on her own, or else her lover will look wimpy.

Vampires

Her fangs tore crimson holes in his neck

Through blood-slicked lips and crimson eyes, the vampires called to her

The vampire moved slow and sensual, stalking his prey with delight

The coffin creaked and a shriveled, corpse-like hand appeared

Her life drained out under his unholy kiss

She was even more beautiful in death than in life

The horrors of the grave were nothing to her now

A smile crossed his lips, revealing ivory fangs and endless hunger

The midnight thirst was upon him

He regarded me with almost human eyes and insatiable hunger

The weird man wanted my blood

Once he had tasted her blood, he could not stop

The sweet nectar pulsed invitingly behind the blue veins of her throat

His throat grew parched at the sight of her pulsing neck

The thing shriveled under the wooden stake's relentless assault

Unable to enter, the creature paced and growled at the threshold

His fangs ached for her throat, to taste the soft flesh and warm blood

His fangs pricked playfully at her neck

His mouth throbbed with the urgent need of his fangs

As soon as his fangs tapped her veins, he knew she was the one

She kissed him and felt his fangs prick her probing tongue

Her lips curled back in anger, revealing the razor-sharp canines

Sunlight burned him, made him a screaming bonfire that fled from us

As he fed, the years tumbled away, restoring the vitality of youth

The blood-hunger made her quiver with anticipation

A cruelty about his eyes and mouth betrayed him as a bloodsucker

His fangs traced the delicate hollow of her neck

The dark juices of that ivory throat would soon be his

Her blood was hot and salty upon his tongue and he gulped greedily

He would have lived forever had he not fallen in love with her

The waxen face drew close, hooded eyes hypnotizing her

We were all reflected in the mirror except her

Deathly pallor crept over her as she drew the curtains against the dawn

A thin rivulet ran down his neck from where her ruby lips had been

He visited her nightly until she was one of us no more, but undead

The veins in her neck sang to him like no other sound on earth

She drew close to him, unaware it was his will she do so

His crimson fangs flexed into her throat, drawing blood

The wooden stake pierced him, holding him prisoner in his coffin

The first gray light of dawn called him to the safety of his tomb

His eyes burned with a feverish light as he sprang from the grave

This vampire fed on youth, not blood, and she stole it with a kiss

The vampire drank her beauty like fine virgin blood

He had the bloodthirsty look in his eyes

He would need to feed soon, to sup on rich, hot blood

His dangerous fanged mouth drifted closer

His fangs nipped at her neck

He nipped at her pulse

He licked the bite marks clean

His eyes rolled back in his head as he drank

His lips were cold, his flesh colder still

His coldness pressed against her

He was cold to the touch

His coldness sent a warning shiver through her

He gave her a slow, sexy bite

His hypnotic red eyes held her

His eyes were scarlet pools of shadow

His snake-like eyes watched her

He forced himself to blink to maintain the illusion of life

He didn't need to breathe, but had perfected the illusion he was alive

The blood-bond let him enter her mind like a thief in the night

He wanted to read her mind and control her

Compelled love was empty love

He quickly discarded those he used—one way or another

He retracted his fangs

He bared his fangs, hissing hate

He wanted her for his immortal bride

He wanted to make her his vampire bride

He wanted to share eternity with her

He had a coffin built for two

He gave her the key to his crypt

He had the raw intensity of immortal passion

Until his bloodlust was aroused, he remained cold, logical

He had the amused look of a man who had seen it all before

He could speak at length about distant times and places

He spoke as if he had actually lived in those times and places

He had a passion for the past, for the history of his people

He had accumulated vast wealth over the centuries

Money was nothing to him, time was nothing—only love mattered

He spent his daylight hours lost in a fog, dreaming of blood

Vampires could be even more territorial than werewolves

He had the arrogance of the undead

His immortal disdain for the living showed

His skin was cool to the touch, but there was crimson fire in his eyes

He had no need to compel this woman who came to him willingly

She must come to him willingly, or not at all

He spoke slowly, thoughtfully, with all the wisdom of the ages

Wasting blood was the worst sin to a vampire

His kiss was like a strange drug, demanding more and more of her

She wanted to be as he was, free and forever young

She fed him on blood when her love was not enough

Her love was the only thing that held his unholy hunger in check

He was as maddeningly arrogant as any man who could cheat death

She was powerless to resist his supernatural charm

Her desire damned her, yet she did not care

She longed for the coming of night and his forbidden embrace

Seeing her now almost made his heart beat again

His bold red eyes brooked no resistance

Heartbroken, she flung herself over his coffin and wept tears of blood

The sound of her beating heart brought him out of the grave

The doom of love at least broke the monotony of the grave

Theirs was a passion that went beyond life and beyond death

He regarded her feminine charms with baleful eyes and brooding lips

That they were together, even now, proved their love was eternal

Theirs was a bond that would last beyond the grave

Her longing for him equaled his lust for blood

She would sacrifice anything to be with him—even her soul

The love she gave was greater than the death he took

Love's power transformed them—from life to death, and death to life

She spilled her bleeding heart upon the altar of his love

Her beauty warmed the ice of his unbeating heart

Her love was the reason he died, and the reason he returned

To find one such as her now was impossible, yet here she was

She had dreamed of a love like his all her life, yet it was doomed

He placed her hand over his heart and she knew he was dead, undead, or something in-between

His thirst, which had once been for blood, was now for her love

He used all the wisdom of his hundred years of unlife to help her

He saw this mortal girl as his redemption

The thought of love with a mortal was almost too painful

How quickly mortal beauty fades, he thought

The dark and dreamy depth of his love frightened her

She followed him down into the crypt and found the truth

Theirs was an unbreakable bond of blood, love, and life everlasting

His longing became hers and together, they shared the cemetery night

Their hungry mouths fed on each other in the darkness

Vampire-like, she sucked and nibbled at his exposed neck

He ignited her soul as no living man could

WITCHES AND WIZARDS (INCLUDES MAGIC)

The wizard stroked his beard and nodded

The wizard cursed and muttered, then glared into the darkness

The air hummed, thick with magic

Magic had rules, but they were not made by man

The wizard laughed and said magic was the science of the gods

The wizard had little interest in the affairs of men

The wizard's eyes lit up when he saw the ancient library

The wizard poured over the dusty tomes and scrolls

What power he possessed died with him, but the dread book remained

The cursed book read like the vile ramblings of a madman

A glow settled upon me and with it, a strange peace

She showed me things I dare not repeat

From out of time and space, the call was heard

Time slowed and sorcery grew thick

The mystic circle throbbed with the sigils of power

The wizard's sigil burned into my brain

The sorceress finished her spell, faded, and was gone

With a wave of his wand, the wizard made the impossible real

Where his glowing staff pointed, death followed

Sorcery flew from her fingers, reducing men to ash

The air was charged with ancient power

Of the names of power, the wizard recited them all

No incantation could save her now

A halo of doom hung over the ensorcelled man's head

She was alive with the unnatural power at her command

She spoke the words that sealed his fate

The air sizzled with sorcery

The sorcerer was well-versed in the Black Arts

— Limits of Magic —

Every fantasy or paranormal romance features some kind of magic, but not every novel has a fully-developed system for how magic works in that world. Magic systems are important because if the author knows the rules, he knows what magic can and can't do.

One of the worst things you can do as an author is invent a magic item or spell that's *too good*. Readers will wonder why the hero (or villain) simply doesn't use it all the time to solve her problems and short-circuit the plot.

The usual workaround is to impose limits on how and when the spell can be cast or item used. These limits must make sense, and there must be a very real and tragic penalty for violating that limit.

Here are some ideas for limitations per use of a spell or item:

- Rare and costly material components or sacrifice of value
- Specific rare event must be occurring (eclipse, etc.)
- Must perform a holy quest, demonic pact, or other action
- Life force drain (premature aging) or worse, *soul drain*
- More than one use causes permanent insanity
- More than one use is impossible (or fatal)

The archmage grew impatient and his apprentice paid the price

The sorcerer cast back his hood, revealing a lined and troubled face

Strange symbols still danced across the enchanted blade

An elementalist could never learn magic of his opposing elements

Such a voyage needed an elementalist versed in air and water magic

The desert tribes practiced pyromancy, the art of conjuring flame

The Cryomancer was the fabled archmage of the Ice Wizards

Reshaping the barren land required the services of a terramancer

The necromancer was clad in robes black as night

The necromancer's bone staff was tipped with a glowing human skull

The necromancer's crypt was foul with a charnel stench

The secrets of the dead were an easy prize for the necromancer

From the tomb, I heard the necromancer's call for me to join him

The dead came back at his command

Necromancy was the foulest of magic

Necromancy corrupted all who practiced its Dark Art

The grinning necromancer made a fist and I felt my heart stop

Slaves to his dark soul, the spirits answered the necromancer's call

Necromancers sought the secret of immortality

Once the wizard placed his soul in the gem, he could not age or die

The immortal wizard decided to claim her as his apprentice

Sex magic bound her to him

His sex magic went beyond any of the tantric practices she'd learned

The witch maintained her youth and beauty through blood magic

The witches danced and the Goddess answered

The witches bid me join them under the moonless sky

The young witch had learned much from her dark mistress

Researching the spell would take precious time she didn't have

The witch was comely, but surely not enough to damn one's soul for

The witch's fingers weaved purple patterns in the moonlight

The spell was almost as insidious as the witch who cast it

A sinister tingling played over her as the witch cast her spell

The Craft was in her blood and in her mother's before her

A wise and cunning woman, she brandished the charm and laughed

The charm burned like fire around my neck

She tossed the wax doll into the fire, where it bubbled and hissed

The man screamed as she pushed the pin into the weird doll

From the bonfire, the old witch cursed us as she died

Black and terrible, the witch's curse rang down through the centuries

The hag died with a half-cast spell lurking upon her lips

The spell's energy crackled into her

The wand's lightning sizzled her soft flesh

The wizard's staff sprayed crimson energy

Orange bolts cut the air *(substitute spell color of your choice)*

Orange death blazed all around *(substitute spell color of your choice)*

— Alpha and Beta Heroes —

An alpha male is strong, ambitious, powerful, and charming. He dominates his environment. A beta is just as charming, but more relaxed and sensitive to others. Both are successful at their jobs.

PART 4

Science Fiction Romance

— Pleasure Beyond Space & Time —

Science Fiction Romance

The alien warrior's sexual stamina far exceeded any earth-man's

The alien warrior's body rippled with muscle

The alien's muscles rippled beneath his blue skin

The alien warriors were perfect specimens of manhood

The alien had been bred for battle, but also excelled at love-making

The alien warrior dedicated the battle to her

The alien battled his lust for her with his mission's priorities

The alien regarded her humanity as primitive and erotic

Here, beyond the stars, she was considered a rare, exotic beauty

The alien had mind-bonded with her

Their mind-bond linked them more closely than mere physical touch

The alien pulled the fantasy from her mind and made it reality

It covered itself in the illusion of what her "perfect man" looked like

Weightless, they made love as the stars drifted by

Their bodies floated as one through the endless night

It was impossible to think she could find love in this strange world

To find love so far away from home had been unthinkable before now

The alien love-bond was for life

He smiled his inscrutable alien smile at her

He had plowed the primitive field of her body and found it fertile

The alien promised to show her all the sights his galaxy had to offer

Time Travel Romance

Love had been the furthest thing from her mind when planning the trip

She had traveled through time to find true love, true happiness

She found his old-fashioned manners refreshing

She had never considered she could find love in the distant past

He found her futuristic thoughts and beliefs wild, reckless

He found her primitive beliefs amusing—and annoying

This was an unhurried time, free from modern distractions

There was time to love here, time to love and be loved

At first, she feared she would never fit in

She'd always had an "old soul" and had found her time at last

She was careful not to do anything that might upset the timeline

With the timeline disturbed, she wasn't sure what she was going back to

She strapped herself into the time machine

Someone had secretly changed the settings on the time machine

She had no idea where she was, either the country or the year

To these Puritan primitives, her time machine was the devil's witchcraft

---

— Writing Effective Action Scenes —

To write effective action, don't go into more detail than you have to, and don't let your characters pause to reflect on what is happening. Would you have time to think or say more than a few words in a real fight? No! Short sentences and paragraphs ratchet up pacing and suspense. Like when our heroine confronts an angry alien mob:

Sarah Conrad drew her blaster and shot into the crowd blocking her from the ship. Bodies hit the dirt. Screaming. Sobbing. Dying.

The remaining aliens panicked. Some ran. Others dove for cover. And one, braver than the rest, returned fire . . .

— Alien Creatures —

AQUATICS

The scaly skin and gills told me it was from a water world

It had the mouth of a lamprey

Its suckered mouth was lined with serrated fangs

The aquatics were small, bluish things that could not breathe our air

The aquatic flesh had a greenish hue

Snake-like, it struck, a whipping mass of tentacles born to kill

The body was barrel-shaped, surrounded by tentacles

It had a squid-like beak capable of cracking through armor

Tentacles wreathed its face and venom lurked in every word

The aquatic spoke in a guttural, half-gargling tone I would have found humorous if it hadn't been pointing a blaster at me

The aquatic's webbed fingers closed over the hilt of its harpoon gun

The aquatic knifed through the water

The aquatic was in its own element now

There was no point chasing an aquatic underwater

The aquatic's finned head turned in my direction

The aquatics were vaguely eel-like, almost boneless in their movement

The aquatic grinned, showing teeth as sharp as needles

The aquatic had to submerge itself every few hours or risk drying out

Its eyes were dead black, like those of a shark, and when it smiled, the resemblance was even stronger

AVIANS

Tufts of scarlet feathers sprang from the man-bird's head

The bird-man beat its wings and cried for blood

The avian flapped its feathered wings

The winged alien flew from its perch

The sinister bird-man hovered before us

It moved on gossamer wings

It spread its wings in a defiant gesture

The alien was black-plumed, with a monstrous twenty-foot wingspan

The alien kept its wings folded carefully against its body

The soft *thwap* of beating wings accompanied the avian's arrival

The avian had a bird-like beak

It spoke our language in a rasping bird-like croak

The avian croaked a warning not to come any closer

With a practiced beak, the avian preened its feathers

The avian's head jerked and bobbed as it examined the area

The avian cawed sharply in alarm

BLOBS

The rubbery blob could stretch itself to fit under doors

The blob extended a pseudopod as if to shake hands

The blob shook with laughter

The blob's brain sat in the center of its see-through body

Four dark spots spaced around the blob's center served as eyes

The blob opened one mouth to talk and another to eat

The blob's skin was dull red until angered, then grew bright

The blob could assume the shape of anyone its own size

A shape-changing blob made the perfect assassin

The blob could transform into whatever creature it ate

It took several minutes for the blob to completely transform

It crawled on its fat belly like a slug, leaving a trail of slime

The living slime oozed forward to feast on human flesh

Inch by inch, the alien slime oozed toward her unprotected skin

The writhing protoplasm gave birth to hungry monsters

The slime formed itself into the semblance of a man

Energy Beings

Energy beings could be distinguished by a slight sheen or haze in the air

Gradually, the translucent glow took on human shape

The energy being danced and shimmered in the dark

Wailing, the space ghost lunged and passed right through me

An icy chill passed over me as the energy being passed though me

Energy beings drew their shapes from their summoner's mind

The energy being offered a telepathic exchange of information

The space demon's true form was pulsing black shadow

The energy being's aura was pure evil, malignant and gloating

The alien's aura was pitch black shot through with pulsing red

Energy beings could possess the living

The aliens were made of energy that needed to possess human bodies

Without host bodies, the alien energies could do nothing

In the mirror, I saw a ghostly form superimposed over my own

The face in the mirror was no longer mine, but that of the alien

The energy being refused to be cast out of the girl

The force possessing her was old, evil, from beyond space and time

My flesh obeyed only the alien now

My will was no longer my own

The energy being was all too eager to live through me, in me

My mind screamed in torment as the alien whispered its commands

The energy being was in me now, controlling me like a puppet

If the energy being had ever been sane, it was only hunger and hate now

The shadow-spirits were comprised of dark, primordial energy

The spirit took offense at being called a mere demon—it was far worse

The energy vampire drained everything it touched

Living shadows drained the life from those who dared enter the ship

The dark spirit offered power and wisdom in exchange for life force

The dark spirit was older than any demon and far more powerful

The spirit claimed to be from the void before the universe existed

The spirits of the void brought with them a chilling cold

The alien spirit spoke only in terms of cold logic and contempt

The alien was some sort of energy being that fed on human suffering

Whatever it was, the energy being was annoyed we had contacted it

Communicating with the alien power was more difficult than I thought

Maintaining the link to the alien spirit's dimension drained him

The alien spirit cared for men as much as men cared for insects

The alien spirit ate memories like men eat meat

This alien seemed interested in our world—perhaps too much

The alien insisted I could not understand unless we became "one"

The weird spirit asked if it could wear my flesh

The alien offered to "relieve me of my hopeless flesh" and free my spirit

Whatever I had contacted, it came from another dimension unlike ours

The alien spirit spoke in a harsh, buzzing drone that filled me with fear

The alien spirits claimed to be gods who ruled where men rule now

The alien spirit demanded to know why I had dared to contact it

Gas-Breathers and Gaseous Beings

The thing sucked pinkish gas through some kind of tube

Oxygen was poison to these beings

They wore breath masks and carried tanks of blue gas

The slow rasp of the alien's filtration system filled the room

Without a working mask, the alien gurgled and died

Deprived of its gas, the alien collapsed in on itself like an inflatable doll

The alien was more mist than man, but no less dangerous

The mist-men's minds were lost to madness and the urge to kill

It flowed forward, fog-like, but with deadly intelligence

It wanted us to breathe it in so it could control us like puppets

The cloud monster killed by engulfing prey in its toxic embrace

The cloud creature poured into her through every orifice

Grays

The aliens were gray-skinned with large heads and black eyes

The black eyes never blinked, just watched remorselessly

Its eyes were almond-shaped and bore a cold intelligence

It had a small, lipless mouth, more like a slit

The Grays had flat faces with nostrils but no nose

The Gray had no visible ears but somehow it heard me

The Grays rarely spoke, preferring to communicate via telepathy

I felt the gray-faced alien probe my thoughts

Cruel and emotionless, the Gray selected a probe from the table

The Grays were imperious, demanding total obedience

The Gray did not care what I wanted, so long as I obeyed

Its intelligence was cold, ruthless, and not of this world

They were cold, logical, and utterly ruthless

They were tall, thin, and wholly evil

The Grays were tall and impossibly thin, possessed of a strange grace

The skeletal aliens reminded me of cosmic reapers

The delicate fingers were long and probing

Its long, spindly arms each ended in three fingers and a thumb

They had black eyes as cold and distant as their home planet

Black and lidless eyes watched our every move

Expressionless, the aliens watched us as if we were no better than bugs

The aliens lacked emotion—even their cruelty was like ice

They were gray-skinned humanoids, thin and regal

They were fascinated with experimenting on humans

The alien spoke to me in my mind

The alien made itself heard in our minds

The alien imposed its will via telepathic command

The aliens were imperious, demanding total obedience

The alien offered me the choice of the probe or the scalpel

INSECTOIDS

The aliens watched me with their bug-like eyes

The alien's stick-like limbs gestured wildly

The razored mandibles clacked for emphasis as it spoke

The alien spoke in a harsh, buzzing tone

Its insect-like mouth chittered and clacked

It waved its antennae in our direction

Its purple eyestalks extended in every direction

Its eyestalks raised in alarm when it saw me

Under its bony shell, the thing was slug-like

Its armored carapace was the dead black of space

Spider-like, the insectoids scuttled toward us

The mantis-men marched on the unsuspecting outpost

The moth-man had multifaceted red eyes

It had a barbed, whip-like tail not unlike a scorpion

It had poison fangs and crushing claws

The sky grew dark with the buzzing of winged insect-men

Its head was crowned by a circle of beady black eyes

The ring of eyes on the insectoid's head watched me

Its expression was impossible to read

Insectoids could see in all directions and were never surprised

Insectoid vision extended into other spectrums, including infrared

They could see only one spectrum at a time, but could change it at will

It wanted to lay its eggs in me

The arachnoids employed polymer web guns to take prisoners

INVADERS (GENERIC)

The aliens came from a parallel dimension

The invasion had not come from the stars, but another dimension

The aliens arrived through dimensional gates

They had come from our doomed future to conquer the past

From out of the dimensional rift, the aliens came

Few in number, the aliens used drones to fight their battles

Microscopic aliens invaded our brains, turning us into puppets

The first spaceships appeared over world capitals

The alien ship hovered over the doomed city

A fleet of warships hung in orbit, poised for conquest

We had no defense against their advanced technology

Alien fighters screamed through the sky

Alien bio-weapons scoured the cities clean of all human life

The aliens seeded the clouds with poison rain

The alien weather machine turned our own planet against us

They intended to strip-mine our planet of its resources—including us

Alien planet-bombs laid waste to the population

We were to be used as slave labor for our alien overlords

Those who collaborated with the aliens were worse than traitors

They were a race built for war

They were a conqueror breed

Mercy was as alien to them as their appearance was to us

The aliens looked nothing like the movies

The invader gazed at her with cold, black eyes

The aliens were strong, powerful, with technology to match

The aliens had a dozen names for war, but none for peace

The aliens offered only slavery or death

The invader cracked its energy whip to demand our obedience

When I failed to obey, the alien frowned and drew its blaster

The aliens were actually mutant humans from the future

Their weird technology was powered by disembodied brains

The aliens harvested human brains, keeping them alive forever

Every alien was connected to the Hive Mind

The aliens' arrogance would be their downfall

The invaders unleashed an EMP that sent us back to the Dark Ages

The alien EMP knocked out the power grid

Without power, we were easy prey for the invaders

Without power, our defenses were crippled

Our dependence on technology had been our undoing

Mammalian

The alien had a flat head and thick neck

The head was spade-shaped, its gold eyes owl-like in their intensity

It had leathery, hairless skin

It resembled a leathery, winged ape

The aliens had translucent, see-through skin revealing their organs

It had thick, trunk-like limbs capable of great strength

The massive alien flexed all four of its arms

Its boneless, three-fingered hands ended in suction cups

It was sleek-furred and catlike with gold, watchful eyes

The alien's ears ended in delicate points

The alien's features were long and thin with immaculate cheekbones

The alien's eyes were rich amber, the color of honey

The alien's curious gold eyes met mine

The alien's hair fell in a shimmering cascade down her back

The alien was beautiful and possessed of an uncompromising grace

The alien's skin was midnight blue, her hair ghostly white

Her blue skin glimmered beneath the twin moons

These aliens were a stout, hardy people who kept to themselves

The people of this world were short and squat, perfect for its low gravity

The alien was surprisingly fast and nimble for one of his size

These aliens were clannish, gruff-tempered

These aliens were dwarf-like and a dour, an uncompromising lot

The aliens were stone gray with dirt-brown horns

The beast-man snuffled at our scent with his piglike snout

The aliens were wolf-like and savage, covered in shaggy fur

The alien's body was man-like, but covered in fur

The alien's green skin was heavily muscled

The green-skinned female danced, bending in ways no human could

The brutes were feral, beast-like: all fang, tusk, and hard muscle

The aliens were savage things, built for war and naught else

Axe raised, the alien came hulking forward

The alien's grin was all yellow fang

These aliens were dull-witted and quick to anger

The little green man leered at her with its beady red eyes

That these were a primitive, backward people, I had no doubt

Their species were world-bound, unaware of our empire

Monsters (Misc.)

The beast stamped the earth with its cloven hooves, then charged

The beast plowed into him, goring him with its horns

The creature hissed and snatched at the girl with its claws

The snow worm was white-furred and savage

It regarded me with almost human eyes and insatiable hunger

The beast was cunning, with the mind of a killer

The monster was all tusk and horn with a disposition to match

All the devils in hell had nothing on this thing

It was a thing born of nightmare and twice as mad

Such a thing should not exist, yet here it was

In its death throes, the mewling creature was almost pitiable

The weird beast wanted my blood

Once it had tasted blood, it could not stop

It was a thing that should not be, yet here it was

The monstrous thing filled me with revulsion

The hungry she-beast's mouth was a vast, sucking hole

It had acid for blood and armor for skin

It had an elongated skull and whiplike tongue

The hungry space vultures devoured derelict ships and crew alike

The giant two-headed space dragon breathed lightning bolts at us

The space dragons had come to feast on our world

This alien mega-lizard put the dinosaurs to shame

The giant space lizard towered over the city skyline

The gargantuan horror loomed over the horizon

It was a behemoth from another world

The colossus stalked forward, bellowing atomic rage

The monstrous space lizard breathed radioactive fire

Reptilians

These aliens were amphibian, equally comfortable on land as in water

The alien's rough-textured skin was chameleon-like

The aliens could alter their skin-color to blend in like chameleons

It was reptilian, with snapping jaws and thrashing tail

The scaled one shrieked and beat its leathery wings

The alien was doglike and scaly

Its scales were impenetrable to our weapons

Green, the serpent man was—the color of poison, the color of death

The serpent man turned his scarlet eyes upon us

The serpent men took up a soft, sibilant whisper

Serpent people could appear as men when they wished

The serpent men were interested in humans only as slaves

The lizard man hissed a warning for us to leave

The lizard man's scales shone iridescent green in the sunlight

The lizard men lived on what fish and wild game they could catch

The lizard men rarely ventured far from their swamp

The lizard man hissed his reply

The alien female slithered forward on her snake-like lower body

The reptilian soldier rubbed lubricating oil over its scales

The reptoid was communicating through pheromones, not sound

The reptoid produced a hypnotic pheromone that compelled us to obey

The aliens resembled a monstrous cross between men and alligators

The gator-man's jaws snapped shut with deadly force

He was half-man, half-dinosaur, with the lustful appetites of both

---

— True Love Comes in Stages —

You can't have your characters fall in love too quickly, or take too long. While lust comes quickly, it may burn out just as fast. True love comes in stages of deepening friendship and emotion forged by bonds of trust and shared experience. In most romances, the first sex scene never comes before page 40 or later than page 150.

— PART 5 —
Words of Passion

— Action Vocabulary —

Acid and Drowning

Bubble, blister, boil, burn, consume, corrode, crumble, dissolve, disintegrate, decay, eat away/into, erode, gush, immerse, inhale, liquify, scald, sear, sizzle, slosh, slop, soak, spill, splash, spurt, submerge

Attack

Abuse, annihilate, assail, assault, attack, besiege, break through, bull rush, charge, conquer, counterattack, cripple, damage, destabilize, destroy, devastate, disable, fall upon, fire, force, glance, graze, harm, hit, hurt, impair, incapacitate, inflict, injure, lame, lay into, lay waste, maim, mar, overcome, overwhelm, pounce on, raze, ruin, rush, sabotage, savage, scatter, set upon, spoil, storm, strike, swoop, traumatize, triumph over, trounce, vanquish, weaken, wound

Biting and Blood-Drinking

Ate, bit, bite, bolt down, breakfast, chew, chomp, chow down, chug, consume, crunch, demolish, devour, dine, drink, eat, fang, feast, feed, gnaw, gobble, gorge, graze, gulp, guzzle, ingest, lunch, munch, nibble, nip, nosh, partake of, pig out on, polish off, put away, quaff, scarf, sip, snack, snap, swallow, swill, swig, sup, tear, tuck into

Crushing

Bang, bash, batter, beat, belt, bludgeon, bop, brain, break, bruise, bounce, bowl over, bump, burst, bust, butt, clout, clobber, collide, crack, crease, crumple, crunch, crush, cuff, dent, flatten, force, fracture, fragment, grate, grind, hammer, hit, impact, kick, knock, mangle, mash, paste, pound, press, pry, pulp, pulverize, pummel, punch, ram, sap, seize, shatter, slam, slap, smash, smack, smite, snap, sock, splinter, squash, squeeze, strike, stun, thump, trample, wallop, whack, wrench

Cutting and Clawing

Bleed, butcher, carve, chop, claw, cleave, clip, crop, cube, cut, cut to pieces/to ribbons, dice, gash, graze, gut, knife, lacerate, mince, mow, mutilate, nick, pincer, rake, rend, rip, saw, scrape, scratch, score, shred, slash, slice, slit, sliver, snip, split, strip, talon, tatter, tear, trim, whittle

Defense

Bar, barricade, beat back, block, bolster, counteract, curb, defend, disallow, disarm, dodge, drive back, end, evade, exclude, fend off, fight off, force back, foil, forbid, forestall, fortify, guard, hamper, halt, hold off, impede, inhibit, interrupt, keep at bay, obstruct, parry, preclude, preempt, prevent, prohibit, proscribe, protect, push back, repel, repulse, resist, restrain, secure, shield, stave off, stop, thwart, ward off

Fire, Electrocution, Energy, and Explosions

Ablaze, aflame, alight, bake, blacken, blast, blaze, blister, blow up, bomb, bombard, bonfire, brand, broil, burn, burst, candle, careen, char, charge, crackle, detonate, discharge, emit, fire, flame, flare, electrify, electrocute, erupt, explode, fly, fly apart, glow, hum, ignite, incinerate, jolt, juice, launch, let fly, let loose, let off, level, light, lit, open fire, pick off, paralyze, ping, ricochet, roar, roast, rocket, sear, scald, scorch, set off, shell, shock, shoot, shrapnel, singe, sizzle, smoke, smolder, spark, stream, streak, surge, vaporize, up in flames, whistle, whiz, whoosh, zap

Killer and Victim Vocalizations

Babble, bark, bawl, bay, beg, bellow, blubber, blurt out, breathe, burble, cackle, call for help, call out, caterwaul, chant, cheer, choke, chortle, chuckle, cough, cry, cry out, curse, exclaim, exhale, gabble, gag, gargle, gasp, gibber, giggle, grate, groan, growl, grumble, grunt, guffaw, gulp, gurgle, holler, hoot, howl, inhale, intone, invoke, jabber, keen, lament, laugh, mewl, moan, mumble, murmur, mutter, plead, purr, rasp, roar, sing, scream, screech, shout, shriek, shrill, sigh, snap, snarl, snicker, snigger, snivel, sob, squeak, strangle, tee-hee, titter, twitter, wail, weep, wheeze, whimper, whine, whisper, whistle, yell, yelp, yowl

Magical and Psychic Attack and Defense

Abjure, activate, affect, afflict, alter, animate, banish, beguile, billow, blast, block, call forth/up, cascade, cast, change, charge, chant, charm, cloud minds, conjure, counter-spell, course through, curse, deactivate, deceive, delude, demoralize, disappear, drain, emit, empower, enchant, energize, engulf, ensorcel, envelop, evoke, fade, flood, flow, fortify, force, frighten, glamor, hex, hypnotize, induce, inflict, influence, inspire, intimidate, invoke, make afraid, make fearful, mesmerize, numb, overwhelm, panic, petrify, polymorph, pour, prey on, radiate, recharge, repel, repulse, roll over, rush, scare, shape, shield, shock, spook, summon, seethe, shower, spiral, steal, swallow up, swarm, swirl, surge, sway, tear the fabric of space/time, teleport, transform, transmogrify, transmute, twist, undulate, vanish, whirl, writhe

Murder and Execution

Assassinate, butcher, croak, cut down, dispatch, dispose of, do away with, do in, eliminate, end, execute, extinguish, exterminate, finish (off), kill, knock off, murder, massacre, poison, neutralize, polish off, put to death, slaughter, slay, take/end life, terminate

Piercing

Bore through, chisel, feed, finger, force, fork, gouge, gore, harpoon, hole, horn, impale, insert, jab, knife, lance, needle, penetrate, perforate, pierce, pin, pincushion, point, poke, plug, punch, prick, puncture, push, run through, skewer, spear, spike, stab, stick, sting, transfix

Bow/Crossbow: aim, click, crank, draw, fire, fix on, fletch, fly, load, loose, nock, notch, pick off, point, rain, restring, release, reload, train, shower, shoot, sight, snipe, storm, strafe, string, target, trigger, volley

Strangling and Fainting

Asphyxiate, black out, choke, choke out, collapse, conk out, cut off air, cut off breath, dizzy, fall unconscious, gag, gasp, go out like a light, gurgle, faint, fight for air, fight for breath, hang, keel over, knock out, light-headed, loss of consciousness, pass out, seize, smother, stifle, strangle, suffocate, swoon, throttle, unsteady, woozy

Violent Release of Bodily Fluids, Guts, and Organs

Barf, bleed, blob, bloom, blossom, boil, bubble, burst, cascade, deluge, discharge, downpour, drain, dribble, drip, drizzle, drool, drop, dump, eject, emanate, empty, escape, evacuate, excrete, explode, extract, exude, filter, flood, flow, flower, fountain, gag, gargle, geyser, glob, glop, gloop, gob, goop, gurgle, gush, heave, issue, jet, leak, ooze, outflow, outpour, plop, pool, pour, puddle, puke, radiate, rain, ralph, ran, release, remove, retch, river, rush, secrete, seep, shot, slime, sluice, slurp, spill, splash, spat, spatter, spew, splatter, spot, spout, spurt, storm, stream, surge, swam, sweat, tear, torrent, trickle, unleash, unload, upchuck, well out/well up from, void, vomit

Violent Removal of Body Parts and Skin

Amputate, behead, came away/off, carve, chop, cut away/off, decapitate, disembowel, dismember, eviscerate, flay, flew away/off, flog, grab, gut, hack, harvest, hew, lash, lop off, pare, part, peel, pluck, pull, prune, pry, remove, rip, scourge, seize, sever, shave, shear, skin, slice, snatch, snip off, strip away, tear away/off, tug, whip, wrench, yank

Body Vocabulary

Where will your lovers kiss, suck, or touch, and in what order? Use this handy list to make your sexy scenes more creative.

HEAD

hair, top of head, forehead, ears, eyebrows, eyelids, corner of eyes, cheek, lips, teeth, tongue, jaw, chin, neck/throat, nape

BODY

collarbone, shoulders, shoulder blades, breasts/pecs, aureolas, nipples, torso, ribs, abdomen/belly/stomach, hips, groin, genitals, back, buttocks

ARMS

biceps, elbows, hands, palms, fingers

LEGS

inner/outer thighs, knees, calves, ankles, feet, toes

Struggling to think of what to call your lovers? Here are some ideas:

MALE DESCRIPTORS

all-male, all-man, brutal, conquering, cruel, dangerous, domineering, hairy, handsome, hard, heavy, male, man, masculine, muscular, possessive, powerful, rigid, rough, savage, strong, thick, vicious, violent, virile

FEMALE DESCRIPTORS

all-woman, beautiful, busty, buxom, creamy, curvy, cute, damp, enchanting, female, feminine, glamorous, glowing, gorgeous, innocent, inviting, perky, pliant, plump, pretty, satin, silk/silky, slender, slim, soft, supple, swaying, undulating, velvet, vivacious, voluptuous, wet, woman

Emotion Vocabulary

Use this vocabulary list whenever you need the perfect word to describe how your character is feeling. This list is mostly for internal emotional states, but does include some external displays such as "red-faced," etc.

AFFECTION

affectionate, compassionate, devoted to, endeared, fond of, fondness, friendly, liking, loving, open hearted, sympathetic, tenderness, warm

ANGER

angry, enraged, furious, hate-fueled, hateful, hostile, incensed, indignant, irate, livid, outraged, resentful

ANNOYANCE

aggravated, annoyed, bedeviled, cross, disgruntled, displeased, exasperated, frustrated, impatient, indignant, irritated, irked, peeved, piqued, riled, teed off, ticked off, vexed

AVERSION

abhorrence of, animosity, antipathy for, appalled, aversion to, contempt, disdain, disgust, dislike, disinclined, distaste for, distrust of, fear of, hatred of, mistrust of, reluctance toward, repulsed, sick of, unwilling, unwillingness

CALM

calm, centered, clear headed, comfortable, content, cool, coolheaded, emotionless, equable, equanimous, even-tempered, fulfilled, grounded, lucid, mellow, nonplussed, phlegmatic, placid, quiet, relaxed, relieved, satisfied, serene, stable, still, tranquil, trusting, unabashed, unemotional, unexcitable, unfazed, unflustered, untroubled

CONFIDENCE

arrogant, assertive, assured, bold, boldness, confident, courageous, determined, empowered, encouraged, open, overconfident, poised, proud, safe, secure, self-assured, self-confident, self-possessed

CONFUSION

addled, ambivalent, at a loss, at sea, baffled, befuddled, bewildered, bemused, clueless, confounded, conflicted, confused, dazed, disoriented, discombobulated, disconcerted, dumbfounded, fazed, flummoxed, hesitant, jumbled, lost, muddle-headed, muddled, mystified, perplexed, puzzled, senile, torn, unbalanced, unhinged

DISCONNECTED

alienated, aloof, apathetic, bored, cold, cut off, detached, disconnected, distant, distracted, divorced from, indifferent, isolated, numb, removed, separated, unavailable, uninterested, withdrawn

EMBARRASSMENT AND REMORSE

apologetic, ashamed, chagrined, conscience-stricken, contrite, crestfallen, distressed, embarrassed, floored, flustered, guilty, humbled, humiliated, mortified, red-faced, self-conscious, shamed, sorry

EXCITEMENT

absorbed, amazed, animated, ardent, aroused, astonished, awed, curious, dazzled, eager, ecstatic, electrified, energetic, enchanted, enraptured, enthralled, enthused, enthusiastic, entranced, excited, exhilarated, exuberant, galvanized, giddy, high, hot, horny, inflamed, incited, inspired, jazzed, lively, motivated, moved, passionate, roused, surprised, thrilled, titillated, turned on, vibrant

FEAR

afraid, anxious, apprehensive, concerned, creeped out, distressed, disturbed, dreading, fear, fearful, foreboding, freaked out, frightened, horrified, jittery, mistrustful, nervous, panicked, paranoid, perturbed, petrified, scared, shivery, stressed out, suspicious, terrified, trepidation, troubled, twitchy, uncomfortable, uneasy, unnerved, unsettled, wary

GRATITUDE

appreciative, beholden, grateful, indebted, moved, obligated, thankful

Hope

assured, buoyant, bullish, encouraged, encouraged, expectant, heartened, hopeful, lighthearted, optimistic, positive, reassured, sanguine, upbeat

Happy

amused, as happy as a clam, beatific, blessed, blithe, blissful, carefree, cheerful, cheery, content, contented, delighted, ecstatic, elated, euphoric, exultant, glad, gleeful, gratified, happy, in a good mood, in good spirits, in seventh heaven, jocular, jolly, jovial, joyous, jubilant, lighthearted, on a high, on cloud nine, on top of the world, overjoyed, pleased, radiant, rapturous, satisfied, sunny, tickled, tickled pink, triumphant, walking on air, well-pleased

Interest

absorbed by/with, alerted, amused by, aroused by, attentiveness, attraction to, concern for, concerned with, curiosity, diverted by, engaged by/with, engrossed in/with, entertained by, enthusiasm for, fascinated by/with, flirted with, gripped by, high regard for, incentivized, inclination, influenced, interested, intrigued, noticed, prompted, regard for, riveted by, stimulated, stirred, tempted by

Love

adored, beguiled by, besotted with, bewitched by, burned for, captivated by/with, carrying a torch for, charmed by, crazy about, desired, doted on, enamored by/with, enchanted by/with, ensorcelled by, entranced by/with, fascinated by/with, hot for, infatuated by/with, mad about, needed, nuts about, passion for, passionate about, smitten with, stuck on, sweet on, taken with, taste for, wanted, wild about

Refreshed

energized, enlivened, fortified, fresh, invigorated, perked up, recharged, re-energized, refreshed, reinvigorated, rejuvenated, replenished, rested, restored, revitalized, revived

Sadness and Pain

afflicted, agony, anguished, bereaved, broken, demoralized, depressed, dejected, despair, despondent, destroyed, devastated, disappointed, discouraged, disheartened, dismal, dismayed, doleful, doomed, forlorn, gloomy, glum, grief, heartbroken, heart-rending, heavy hearted, hopeless, hurt, inconsolable, lonely, melancholy, miserable, mournful, pathetic, pitiful, plagued, regretful, remorseful, rueful, sad, sadness, shattered, sorrow, sorrowful, suffered, suffering, tormented, tortured, unhappy, woebegone, wretched

Surprise

alarmed, discombobulated, disconcerted, disturbed, flustered, perturbed, rattled, ruffled, shaken, shocked, startled, surprised, taken aback, thrown off balance, upset

Tense

agitated, antsy, anxious, apprehensive, at the breaking point, cranky, disquieted, distressed, distraught, edgy, fidgety, forced, frazzled, ill at ease, impatient, irritable, jittery, jumpy, keyed up, neurotic, nervous, on edge, overwrought, panicky, pushed, pushed too far, restless, squirrelly, strained, stressed, stressed out, strung out, twitchy, worked up, worried

Tired

beat, blah, bland, bone-tired, bored, bushed, burnt out, depleted, done in, drained, dull, encumbered, enervated, exhausted, fatigued, jaded, knocked out, lethargic, listless, no energy, overburdened, overloaded, overtaxed, overwhelmed, pooped, ready to drop, sapped, sick of, sleepy, stretched, taxed, tired, tuckered out, uninspired, unoriginal, wasted, weakened, weary, whipped, wiped out, worn down, worn out, zonked

Vulnerable

fragile, guarded, helpless, insecure, leery, reserved, sensitive, shaky

Yearning

ambitious, avaricious, burning, craving, desiring, envious, greedy, jealous, longing, needful, needing, nostalgic, passion, pining, seeking, striving, wanting, wistful, yearning

Love's Coloring Book

By mixing colors with other words or doubling-up similar shades, you can quickly come up with powerful descriptions, such as "the October sky was ghoul-gray" or "the starless night was steeped in shadow."

Black

Anthracite, black pearl, blue-black, coal, crow, dark, dead, ebony, ink, jet, midnight, moonless, night, obsidian, onyx, pitch, raven, sable, shadow, starless, Stygian, subterranean, tenebrous, void, unlit

Blue

Air Force, azure, baby, cerulean, cobalt, cornflower, electric blue, delft, federal, ice, indigo, lapis lazuli, marine, midnight blue, navy, neon, ocean, peacock, periwinkle, powder, Prussian, robin's egg, royal, sapphire, sea-blue, sky, slate blue, sorrowful, steel, teal, turquoise, ultramarine, wedgewood

Brown/Beige

Bay, brick, bronze, brunette, buckskin, café au lait, caramel, chestnut, chocolate, cinnamon, cocoa, coffee, copper, drab, dun, earth, ecru, fawn, foxy, ginger, hazel, henna, khaki, mahogany, maple, mocha, mud, mushroom, nut brown, nutmeg, pecan, raisin, roan, rosewood, saddle, sepia, tan, tanned, taupe, tawny, toffee, tortoise shell, umber, walnut

Gray

Ashen, bleak, charcoal, cloudy, dismal, dove, drab, dreary, dull, gloomy, grizzled, gunmetal, hoary, iron, murky, overcast, pearl, sickly, silver, slate gray, smoky, sooty, somber, stone, sunless, tattletale, tombstone

Green

Aqua, aquamarine, bluish-green, celadon, chartreuse, emerald, envy, forest, grassy, hunter, jade, jealous, kelly, leaf, lime, malachite, mist, mold, moss, olive, pea, pine, sea-green, verdant

Orange

Amber-orange, apricot, atomic tangerine, bittersweet, burnt orange, carrot, champagne, coral, deep carrot, flame, lion, orange peel, orange-red, peach, pumpkin, safety orange, sunset, tangelo, tangerine

Purple

Açai, amaranth, amethyst, aubergine, azurite, blackberry, bluebell, crocus, eggplant, electric purple, frostbite, fuchsia, heliotrope, hibiscus, imperial, indigo, lavender, lilac, lotus, magenta, mauve, orchid, pinot noir, plum, psychedelic, royal, thistle, Tyrian, violet, wisteria

Red/Pink

Apple, auburn, beet, blood, brass, brick, burgundy, candy apple, cardinal, carmine, cerise, cherry, cinnamon, cinnabar, claret, cochineal, crimson, currant, dusky rose, fire, fire engine, fulvous, garnet, hellish, lobster, maroon, ox-blood, raspberry, red amber, rose, rosy, rubescent, rubicund, ruddy, ruby, russet, rust, salmon, sanguine, scarlet, shrimp, strawberry, terra cotta, Titian, Tyrian, tomato, vermeil, vermilion, wine

White/Off-White

Alabaster, anemic, bleached, bloodless, chalk, colorless, cream, deathly, drained, drawn, ecru, eggshell, ghostly, ivory, lily, magnolia, milky, milky quartz, moon, moonstone, oatmeal, opal, oyster, pale, pallid, parchment, pasty, peaked, pinched, salt-and-pepper, snow, vanilla, virgin, wan, washed out, waxen, white jade

Yellow/Gold

Amber, ash blonde, blonde, brass, burnished, buff, cadmium, daffodil, flaxen, fool's gold, fulvous, golden, honey, lemon, jaundiced, jonquil, mustard, palomino, platinum, primrose, sallow, sandy, silver-blonde, straw, tawny, wheat, white-gold

— Colors Writing Exercise —

Experiment with your own combinations. Feel free to mix-and-match colors (e.g., yellow and brown could be combined as "Her *wheat-colored* hair fell in waves over slim, *tanned* shoulders").

— Titles and Terms —

Some titles are invented, others are from different cultures. Alternate titles or definitions are in brackets. Feminine versions are in parentheses.

CRIMINALS (SOME TITLES IMPLY SPECIALIZATION IN CERTAIN TYPES OF CRIME)

Adulterer, apostate, assassin, baddy, bandit, blasphemer, bootlegger, brigand, buccaneer, burglar, cat burglar, charlatan, cheat, chiseler, convict, criminal, crook, culprit, cutpurse, delinquent, embezzler, felon, fence, footpad, forger, fornicator, fraud, fraudster, freebooter, fugitive, gangster, goon, heretic, highwayman, hoaxer, hood, hoodlum, hooligan, imposter, killer, kin-slayer, knight of the road, lawbreaker, malefactor, malfeasant, marauder, misbeliever, miscreant, mobster, mountebank, mugger, murderer, oath-breaker, offender, outlaw, pirate, quack, robber, rustler, sham, shark, sharp, sinner, smuggler, swindler, thief, thug, tough, traitor, trickster, vandal, villain, wrongdoer

GOVERNMENT TYPES

Anarchy, archclericy, autocracy, bureaucracy, caliphate, commonwealth, city state, confederation or confederacy, county, democracy, dictatorship, domain, dominion, duchy, earldom, federation, free city, empire, emirate, hegemony, hierarchy, kingdom, league, march, oligarchy, palatine, patriarchy (matriarchy), plutocracy, prelacy, principality, protectorate, realm, regency, regime, republic, see [holy see], state, sultanate, suzerainty, theocracy, union

Most baronies, counties, duchies, earldoms, marches, principalities, sees, and viscounties will be part of a larger feudal kingdom or empire; however, some may be sovereign nations. Current real world examples are the Grand Duchy of Luxembourg, the Principality of Monaco, and the Vatican City State.

LOVERS

Amour, angel, bae ["before anyone else"], beau, beloved, betrothed, boo, darling, dear, dearest, dear heart, honey, inamorato (inamorata), love, lover, my love, my pet, paramour, pet, sweet, sweetheart

Nobles

Archbaron (archbaroness), baron (baroness), baronet (baronetess), caliph (calipha), chieftain, count (countess), czar (also caesar, kaiser, tsar; czarina, tsarina), duke (duchess), dictator, emir, emperor (empress), esquire, grand duke (grand duchess), headman, khan, king (queen), knight (dame, lady)/knight bachelor/knight banneret, leader, lord (lady), maharaja, majesty, margrave, marquess/marquis (marchioness/marquise), mogul, monarch, overking, overlord, pasha, potentate, prince (princess), rajah, ruler, shah, sheikh, sovereign, sultan (sultana), suzerain, tyrant, viscount (viscountess), warlord

Noble Honorifics

Overking, Emperor: Imperial Majesty

Caliph, King, Sultan, Pasha: Majesty

Archcleric, Duke Palatine, Grand Duke, Prince Palatine, Shah, Theocrat: Royal Highness ["Divine Highness" for religious nobles]

Ambassador, Hierarch, Prince, Count Palatine, Prelate: Highness

Archbaron, Khan, Margrave, Marquis: Noble Grace

Baron, Emissary, Lord Mayor, Magistrate, Viscount: Lordship

Baronet: Sir (Lady)

Lord: Worship

Mayor: Honor

Knight Banneret, Knight Bachelor: Sir (Dame)

A "lord" is also a baron, at minimum, but may have a higher noble title attached, such as a count, duke, earl, marquess/marquis, or viscount. A lordship is always in relation to either a family or territorial name. As such, a lord may be introduced as "Baron Varney Vexham," or "Baron Varney Vexham, Lord of the Black Coast" as the situation warrants. Some younger children of lords not destined to inherit their parent's title may receive a family-related lordship as a *courtesy title* rather than a true peerage. In this case, the territorial title goes to the first born son.

Knighthoods are not hereditary, though baronets are despite neither being members of the nobility. They are considered gentlemen, with the right to be called, "Sir," own estates, and hold various other privileges. These are typically the highest rank to which commoners may rise.

A knight bachelor is usually referred to simply as a knight. They always fight under the banner of another noble. A knight banneret (often called a banneret) always fights under his own banner and is therefore of higher rank than a knight bachelor.

When addressing a noble directly, place "your" before the title, as in "Yes, your Lordship," except in the case of a baronet or knight for whom "Yes, Sir," is correct.

When formally referring to a noble indirectly, place the gender possessive pronoun before the title, as in "His Lordship," except in the case of a baronet or knight. These are introduced as "Sir" ("Dame" or "Lady" for a female), then their name and any other titles held (e.g.: "Sir Charles Chenwyth, Baronet of Bedlamshire."). If they also hold a clerical or military rank, then that rank goes before the "Sir" (e.g.: Captain Sir Charles Chenwyth, Baronet of Bedlamshire").

If referred to casually among peers, male nobles of any rank are always introduced by their first name (e.g.: "Sir Charles"), *never* the last (e.g.: "Sir Chenwyth"). In a traditional feudal society, wives and daughters are addressed by their husband's or family's surname (e.g. "Lady Chenwyth"). To avoid confusion when there is more than one female with that surname, her first name may be mentioned (e.g.: Lady Clara Chenwyth, or "Clara, Lady Chenwyth").

OFFICES

Offices are differentiated by high or low status. High office holders will be drawn from the upper class and nobility, while low office holders will come from the middle and upper lower class.

Some offices are filled by bribery or nepotism. As a result, some officers are corrupt or incompetent to varying degrees. Since few of these offices pay well, it is understood that a fair portion of an officer's income must be derived from embezzling, taking bribes, confiscating property, levying fines, etc. There is a flip side, however: those who become too corrupt or too moral risk attracting important enemies.

HIGH OFFICE HOLDERS

Admiral, alderman, ambassador, bailiff, burgher (burgess), burgomaster, chancellor, commander, consul, director, emissary, envoy, factor, general, field marshal, general, governor, grand admiral, lord high sheriff, justice, legate, lord mayor, magistrate, minister, praetor, premier, prime minister, president, nuncio, plenipotentiary, regent, secretary, senator, shogun, steward, superintendent, viceroy

LOW OFFICE HOLDERS

Assemblyman, attaché, chamberlain, commissioner, congressman, counselor, delegate, herald, inspector, judge, mayor, representative, sheriff, tribune

Priests

Abbot, (abbess), acolyte, adept, anointed, ascetic, archbishop, archcleric, archdeacon (archdeaconess), archdruid (archdruidess), archpriest (archpriestess), ayatollah, bishop, cantor, cardinal, chaplain, churchman, cleric, clergyman (clergywoman), cultist, deacon (deaconess), dean, devotee, disciple, druid (druidess), ecclesiastic, exarch, father (mother), father superior (mother superior), friar, godman, god-speaker, guru, hazzan, hierarch, hierophant, high priest (high priestess), imam, inquisitor, man (woman) of the cloth, metropolitan, minister, monk (nun), mufti, mullah, murshid, mystic, novice, pastor, patriarch (matriarch), pope (papess), preacher, prelate, priest (priestess), primate, prior (prioress), prophet, rabbi, rector, saint, sangha, shaman, swami, theocrat, vicar, vicar general

Priestly Honorifics

Archcleric, Archpriest, Ayatollah, Patriarch, Pope: Holiness

Cardinal: Eminence

Archbishop: Excellency

Bishop: Most Reverend

Abbott: Right Reverend

Prelate: Reverend Monsignor

Abbot, Prior: Reverend Father (Reverend Mother/Sister)

Monk (Nun): Brother (Sister)

Sample Priestly Honorifics

Divinity, Exaltedness, Mercy, Radiance, Reverence, Serenity

As with nobles, when formally referring to a priest indirectly, place the gender possessive pronoun before the title, as in "His Eminence," except in the case of a monk or nun. These are introduced as "Brother" or "Sister," then the first name.

Religious and/or Secret Organizations

Brothers (sisters) of, cabal, chosen of, church, circle, creed, cult, faith/faithful, followers of, order, path of/to, sect, religion, school, seekers of, temple of, tradition, way

Psychics

Diviner, fortune teller, medium, mentalist, mind-bender, mind-mangler, mind-master, mindreader, oracle, psychic, seer, spirit-talker, spirit-walker, spiritualist

Sailors and Ferrymen

Bargeman, boatman, buccaneer, captain, ferryman, freebooter, gondolier, hands, mariner, pirate, privateer, (old) salt, sea dog, seafarer, seaman, skipper, swab/swabby, whaler, voyager

Scientists and Philosophers

Academic, authority, doctor, expert, guru, inventor, learned one, master of, philosopher, professor, preceptor, sage, savant, scholar, scientist, teacher, thinker, thought-giver, wise man (woman)/wise one

Warriors

Archer, band, blade master, bodyguard, centurion, champion, combatant, company, constable, crossbowman, crusader, defender, duelist, fighter, footman, free-blade, freebooter, free-sword, gang, GI, gladiator, gunny, guard, guardian, grunt, hero, horseman, infantryman, jailer, keeper, man-at-arms, marine, merc, mercenary, myrmidon, peacekeeper, pikeman, pit fighter, protector, ranger, sell-sword, sentry, sentinel, serviceman, servicewoman, slinger, soldier, sword master, troop, trooper, warden, warder, warrior, watchman

Army or Navy ranks (commissions) may be bought in some settings, similar to the old British Empire. Some warriors must be voted into their rank by popular consensus of the group they lead, such as bandits, mercenary companies, and pirate crews.

Crewmembers

Away party/away team, captain, chief, co-pilot, commander, crewman/crewmember/crewperson, engineer, first officer, hands, helmsman, maintenance crew, medical officer, navigator, pilot, science officer, security detail, security officer, ship's complement, wingman

---

— True Beauty Is Never Skin Deep —

While couples should be physically attractive in one or more ways, there must be more compelling reasons than that to fall in love (mind, humor, ambition, compassion, etc.). Note that "physically attractive" does not mean your characters can't have scars, birthmarks, or other defects or disabilities. In fact, they should have *at least one* physical, mental, and/or emotional shortcoming which they must learn to accept or correct. Preferably, these shortcomings (or their own negative perception of them) provide some of the reasons why they have not found true love before.

About the Author

Jackson Dean Chase brings you Bold Visions of Dark Places. He is the #1 bestselling author of over twenty fiction, poetry, and nonfiction books for writers, including *How to Start Your Novel*, *How to Write Realistic Characters*, and the *Fantasy Writers' Phrase Book*.

Thanks for buying my book!

If you enjoyed it, please leave an online review. Even if it's just a few lines, your words will make a difference to help me reach new readers.

Have a question or suggestion? Or just want to say hi?

Jackson loves to connect with his fans! Friend or follow him online.

- **Website:** JacksonDeanChase.com
- **Facebook:** facebook.com/jacksondeanchase
- **Tumblr:** JacksonDeanChase.tumblr.com
- **Twitter:** @Jackson_D_Chase
- **Email:** jackson@jacksondeanchase.com

Want to know when Jackson's next book is coming out?

Sign up and get **FREE BOOKS** at: **www.JacksonDeanChase.com**

There's NO SPAM, and your email address will never be sold or shared.

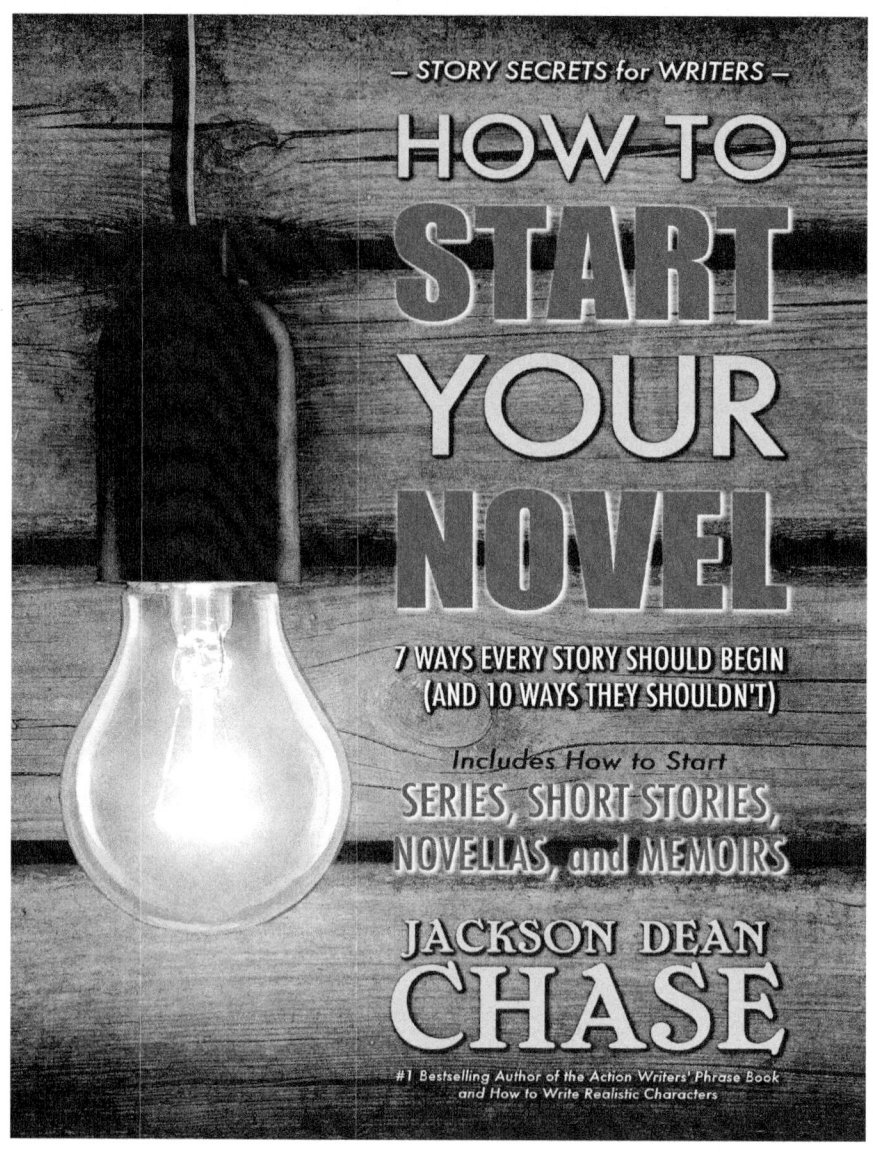

The first words on the page are the hardest you'll write. It's easy to get overwhelmed. **How do bestselling authors do it?** That's what I set out to discover. I tore apart my library, scouring the openings to hundreds of novels to see what makes them work and *why*. And do you know what I found? A pattern—**a secret formula** authors use time and time again to deliver **powerful, bestselling results!**

– SNEAK PREVIEW –
How to Start Your Novel
(excerpt from the chapter on starting with dialogue)

Dialogue puts you into the mouth of a character with something brief and important to say. It can't be, "Hello, how are you?" or "Please, sit down." Anything normal is the kiss of death. Dialogue must be powerful and, like action, it must refer to something exciting that either has happened, is happening, or is about to happen, so make sure there is at least a hint of mystery or danger in your words.

> "We should head back," Gared urged as the woods began to grow dark around them. "The wildlings are dead."
>
> —George R. R. Martin, *A Game of Thrones*

We get an immediate sense of peril, and know that there has been a battle, yet some greater danger remains. What is it? We cannot help but find out. Also, notice how the author mentions the darkening forest between the dialogue. That helps set the scene . . . and the danger.

> "Do the dead frighten you?" Ser Waymer Royce asked with just the hint of a smile.
>
> Gared did not rise to the bait. He was an old man, past fifty, and he had seen lordlings come and go. "Dead is dead," he said. "We have no business with the dead."

These next paragraphs introduce another character, Ser Waymer Royce, and create conflict between him and Gared. They also sketch in a few details about the speakers. More importantly, they both keep talking about the dead. By placing such importance on them, we begin to feel uneasy. It's getting dark. The men are in a forest. Night is falling. This is a medieval fantasy world, so it stands to reason there are a lot of superstitions about the dead coming back to life, not to mention ghosts, curses, that sort of thing.

> "Are they dead?" Royce asked softly. "What proof have we?"
>
> "Will saw them," Gared said. "If he says they are dead, that's proof enough for me."
>
> Will had known they would drag him into the quarrel sooner or later. He wished it had been later rather than sooner. "My mother told me that dead men sing no songs," he put in.

The conversation continues, now bringing in a third minor character, Will, who is the hero of this prologue. By saving Will's reveal for last, we get a chance to peer inside his thoughts for a moment before he speaks. This serves two purposes: 1) it breaks up the conversation which helps pacing; and 2) it sheds some light on Will before he ever opens his mouth. By going inside his head and not into the heads of Gared or Royce, we know Will is more important to the story. We establish him as the hero.

Could Will have spoken first? Sure, but sometimes it's better to hold the hero back so he's already been set up by others and the situation clearly established. That frees the hero's introduction from unnecessary clutter.

> "We have a long ride ahead of us," Gared pointed out. "Eight days, maybe nine. And night is falling."
>
> Ser Waymer Royce glanced at the sky with interest. "It does that every day about this time. Are you unmanned by the dark, Gared?"

Danger is again threatened by the mention of night, then dismissed. It's important to have one character who refuses to heed the warning, who is more interested in scoring points via insults or witty remarks. This creates conflict, but it also ramps up suspense.

Note that some questions lead to monologue instead, with the other characters reflecting on their feelings. It's also a valuable opportunity to weave in details that have no place in dialogue:

> Will could see the tightness around Gared's mouth, the barely suppressed anger in his eyes under the thick black hood of his cloak. Gared had spent forty years in the Night's Watch, man and boy, and he was not accustomed to being made light of. Yet it was more than that. Under the wounded pride, Will could sense something else in the older man. You could taste it, a nervous tension that came perilous close to fear.

We need Gared's reaction, but we don't need to jump into his head to get it. By seeing his reaction through Will's eyes, we stress Will's importance. Gared takes on a mentor role, and Royce continues to be the immediate villain. We also get more suspense as Will notices Gared's fear . . .

Want to find out the best ways to begin your story with action, dialogue, mystery, and more? Get the full book now!

How to Start Your Novel

The 7 Ways Every Story Should Begin
(and 10 Ways They Shouldn't)

eBook and Trade Paperback available now

Writing Romantic Suspense?

Tired of your imagination hitting a brick wall? Pump up your mental muscles with the *Action Writers' Phrase Book*. With over 2,000 ways to describe weapons, fights, and more, it's the perfect workout for authors of Action, Adventure, and Thrillers!

eBook and Trade Paperback available now

Sneak Preview:
This Time, It's Personal

Her red nails raked his cheek, clawing for his eyes

Hairy knuckles crashed home, knocking her senseless

He circled his opponent like a shark smelling blood

The sword swung in savage fury

The blade felt good in his hand, as did the deaths that followed

Gunfights and Bullet Hits

Flesh and brains erupted in a liquid halo

A dozen figures cut through the brush, guns blazing

The shotgun painted the wall a savage red

Explosions and Fiery Doom

Hellfire roared, bringing damnation and death

Red, yellow, and orange: these were the colors of my hate

A living torch, the man ran to the cliffs and fell to the rocks below

Mechanized Death

A madman sat behind the wheel, his brain humming death

The child became a bloody smear across my windshield

The cars crashed in a grinding shriek

ACTION
WRITERS' PHRASE BOOK

eBook and Trade Paperback available now

NEW BY JACKSON DEAN CHASE

BLAST THROUGH WRITER'S BLOCK!

SCIENCE FICTION
WRITERS' PHRASE BOOK

ESSENTIAL REFERENCE for All Authors of SCI-FI, CYBERPUNK, DYSTOPIAN, SPACE MARINE, and SPACE FANTASY ADVENTURE

JACKSON DEAN CHASE

Bestselling Author of *How to Start Your Novel*

Exclusive Sneak Preview:

Planets, Moons, and Asteroids

This was a water world, but like no ocean I had ever seen

The asteroid's surface was pitted and cracked, covered in minerals

A ring of ghost ships orbited the Death Moon

Space Stations

The station's halls were a uniform white, punctuated by black doors

The station was oddly organic-looking in a way that disturbed me

Blast-proof doors came down to seal us in

Starships

The gray bulk of the cruiser drifted by

The imperial flagship loomed ahead, weapons locked

The science vessel scanned the planet's surface for signs of life

Science Fiction
Writers' Phrase Book

eBook and Trade Paperback available now

Printed in Great Britain
by Amazon